Measurement Motivators

by
Thomas J. Palumbo

illustrated by Bron Smith

Cover by Bron Smith

Copyright © Good Apple, Inc., 1989

ISBN No. 0-86653-500-4

Printing No. 987654321

Good Apple, Inc.
Box 299
Carthage, IL 62321-0299

Introduction

Measurement Motivators stresses the integration of measurement with all phases of the mathematics and school curriculum. It emphasizes:

- Activities that teach basic measurement skills
- Techniques for understanding small and large numbers
- Learning devices that better measurement understanding
- Strengthening measurement vocabulary through games/puzzles
- Cross curriculum, short-term measurement projects
- Student research in measurement
- Teaching time-savers
- Board games for concept reinforcement
- Creative people in measurement exploration
- Measurement history
- Classroom interaction with everyday measures
- Practical approaches in problem solving/critical thinking
- Challenging multi-level math/measurement drills
- A variety of out-of-classroom experiences

The reproducible pages, step-by-step directions, student follow-ups, and learning extenders will make the teaching of measurement enjoyable for you and your students.

Dedication

To Thomas Willson Dibble and Allesan Palumbo . . . may they grow up to be great measurers.

Other books by Tom Palumbo include:

GA648 Tuesday Timely Teasers
GA649 Wednesday Midweek Winners
GA650 Thursday Think Time
GA1050 Language Arts Thinking Motivators

GA1095

Table of Contents

GA1095

Measuring the Majestic

Mural Directions

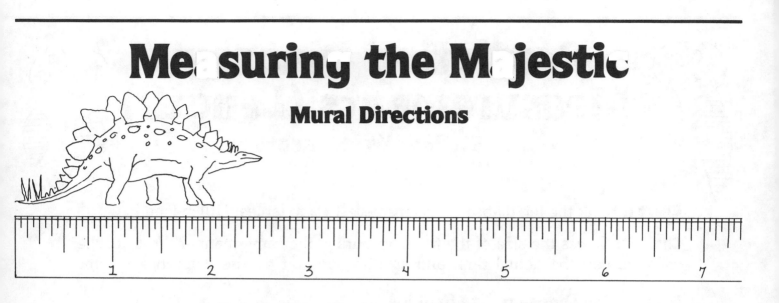

Before beginning the Dinosaur Dimensions activities that follow, place a clear piece of plastic or teacher transparency over the dinosaurs that surround this page. Trace the dinosaurs with a thin black permanent magic marker. Place this transparency on an overhead projector. Tape large pieces of construction paper to the wall. Enlarge the small drawings to fit the paper on the wall. Use your imagination with these giant drawings to create a hall or classroom mural or:

1. Make a cave wall mural.
2. Make a measurement evolution lineup from dinosaur to man.
3. Place comparative drawings of our present day giant animals next to the dinosaurs.
4. Design a zoo with natural settings for the dinosaurs.
5. Place customary or metric measures on your dinosaurs.
6. Place a dinosaur data base under each dinosaur.

1

Predicting Dinosaur Measurements (Length)
Student Work Sheet

Chart I: Rank the ten dinosaurs from smallest (1) to largest (10) in length.

Chart II: Guess the size of the ten dinosaurs in the same manner. Your teacher will give you the actual rank and size so you can do the difference column.

I. Guessing Dinosaur Size Ranking

Dinosaur	Rank Guess	Actual Rank	Difference
Deinonychus			
Silvisaurus			
Brachiosaurus			
Saltopus			
Allosaurus			
Stegosaurus			
Barosaurus			
Diplodocus			
Tyrannosaurus			
Oviraptor			
		Total	

Your teacher will give you the order before starting this chart.

II. Guessing Dinosaur Length

Dinosaur	Length Guess	Actual Length	Difference
		Total	

GA1095

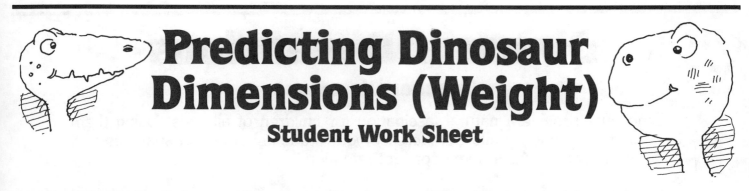

Predicting Dinosaur Dimensions (Weight)
Student Work Sheet

Chart I: Rank the ten dinosaurs below from smallest (1) to largest (10) in weight. Find the difference (guess to rank).

Chart II: Guess the weight of the dinosaurs in the same manner. Your teacher will provide you with the actual measure after your guesses are complete. Find the difference between your guess and the actual weight.

I. Guessing Dinosaur Weight Ranking

Dinosaur	Rank Guess	Actual Rank	Difference
Deinonychus			
Silvisaurus			
Brachiosaurus			
Saltopus			
Allosaurus			
Stegosaurus			
Barosaurus			
Diplodocus			
Tyrannosaurus			
Oviraptor			

II. Guessing Dinosaur Weight

Dinosaur	Weight Guess	Actual Weight	Difference

GA1095

Dinosaur Dimensions
Teacher Directions

Dinosaurs provide a natural fascination for children of all ages. Using them in your measurement units will increase your students' attention spans as well as promote basic measurement concept retention.

Hand out the work sheet or place the ten dinosaur names on the chalkboard in a chart such as the following: (See work sheet.)

Dinosaur	Guess	Actual Rank	Difference
1.			
2.			
3.			
4.			

Tell your students that they are to try to guess which dinosaur is the smallest by placing a one (1) in the *guess* column next to their choice; second smallest receives a two (2); third, three (3); etc. The largest, in their estimation, will receive a ten (10). After the class has made their guesses, tell them the smallest dinosaur and have them put a one (1) next to that dinosaur in the *actual rank* column. Show your class how to record the difference between their guess and the actual rank of the dinosaur. The answer to that easy subtraction problem is then placed in the *difference* column. Do the second and third largest computation with your class. They should be able to complete the rest on their own. If you put the dinosaurs on movable strips of oaktag, the next part of the lesson will be easier. Adding the ten differences will tell the best guessers.

Ask the class if they would like to try to guess the size of each *dinosaur.* Then record the information in the chart below in the same manner as the ranking chart.

Dinosaur	Size Guess	Actual Size	Difference
1.			
2.			
3.			
4.			

Guessing the size of the smallest dinosaur followed by the largest dinosaur, second smallest followed by the second largest helps narrow the guesses and shows the class good problem-solving skills. The subtraction skills in the second chart are more difficult. If your class is not at this level, they can use the difference column to tell whether their guesses were too high or too low. Doing one at a time and then telling the correct answer builds the suspense of who was a good measurement guesser. Repeat this procedure for dinosaur weight.

GA1095

Dinosaur Dimensions
Fact Sheet

	Dinosaur	Name Meaning	Length (feet)
1.	Saltopus	Leaping Foot	2
2.	Oviraptor	Egg Stealer	6
3.	Deinonychus	Terrible Claw	10
4.	Silvisaurus	Forest Lizard	13
5.	Allosaurus	Other Lizard	36
6.	Stegosaurus	Roof Lizard	40
7.	Tyrannosaurus	Tyrant Lizard	50
8.	Brachiosaurus	Arm Lizard	80
9.	Barosaurus	Heavy Lizard	85
10.	Diplodocus	Double Beam	90

	Dinosaur	Weight Length	Weight (pounds)
1.	Saltopus		3
2.	Oviraptor		40
3.	Deinonychus		150
4.	Silvisaurus		2500
5.	Allosaurus		3000
6.	Stegosaurus		4000
7.	Tyrannosaurus		14,000
8.	Brachrosaurus		150,000
9.	Barosaurus		70,000
10.	Diplodocus		25,000

Divide the weight by the length and you can figure the weight per foot. This is a good activity for the upper grades.

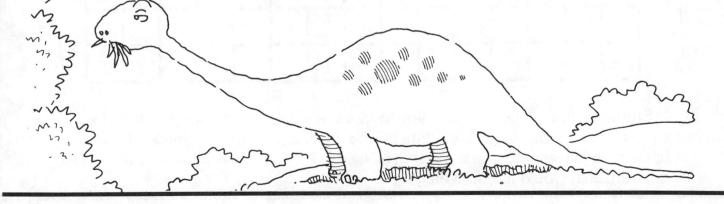

GA1095

Dinosaur Graphs

Each box below is 5 feet by 5 feet. Select five of the ten dinosaurs discussed and draw them, using the scale on this chart.

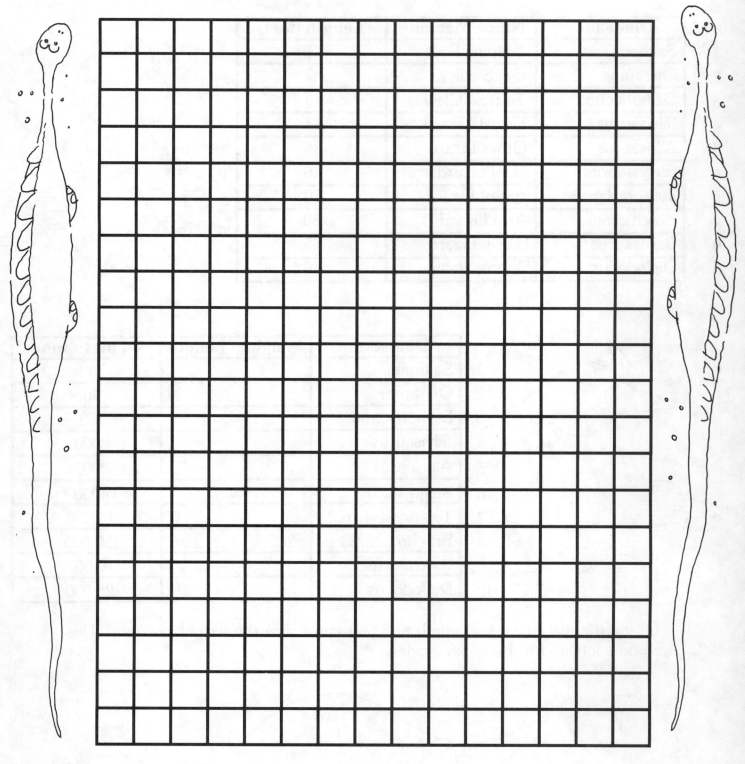

Student Hint: If you would like to draw a different category, change each square to the following: 1 centimeter for insects, 1 inch for birds, 1 foot for basketball players, 10 yards for sports' fields, 1 mile for mountains or any other measure that would fit your category.

6

Dimensions
Blank Master

Use the chart below to compare the sizes of your favorite horses, flowers, basketball players, cars, pets or structures. Develop a unique theme of your own that has not been given much thought. Surround your chart with illustrations or pictures of your theme.

Theme name_____

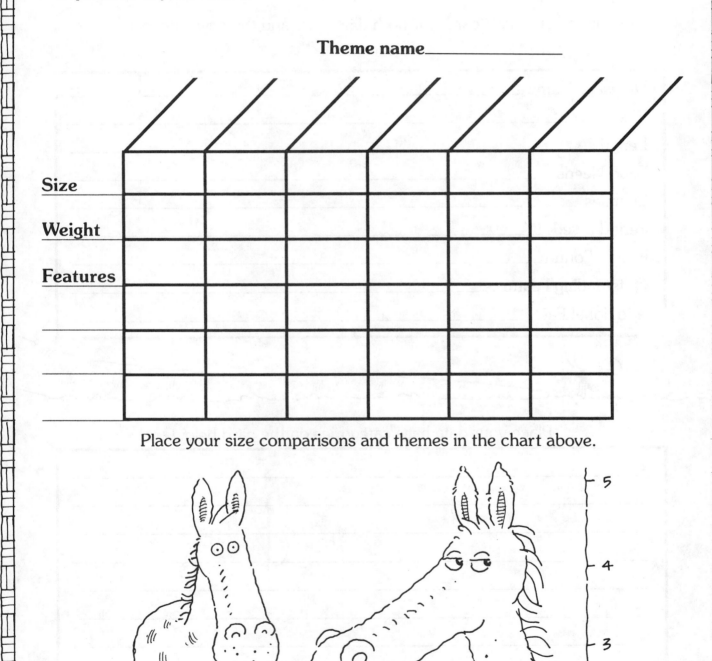

Size

Weight

Features

Place your size comparisons and themes in the chart above.

GA1095

Dinosaur Data Base

Sixty-five million years ago dinosaurs roamed the earth. Present day fossil discoveries and analyses have given us a fairly accurate account of many of them. Creating a data base of facts you found out about dinosaurs will save future students hours of research time. Can you fill in the data base for five dinosaurs and then form a team of five students with similar interests? Pick a theme and create an original data base after completing the one below. Can you suggest other measurement-related data bases to your teacher?

Combine your team's cards for both dinosaurs and the new category.

Dinosaur Name _____

Weight _____

Length _____

Food Needs _____

Enemies _____

Period Lived _____

Fossils Found _____

Outstanding Features _____

Additional Facts _____

Place your data base categories on the card below.

GA1095

Famous Measurements I
Student Work Sheet

Below the picture of each famous structure you will find two measurements. Put a check mark next to the correct answer. Color in each one that you get correct. Design your own Famous Measurements on the next page.

1. Eiffel Tower

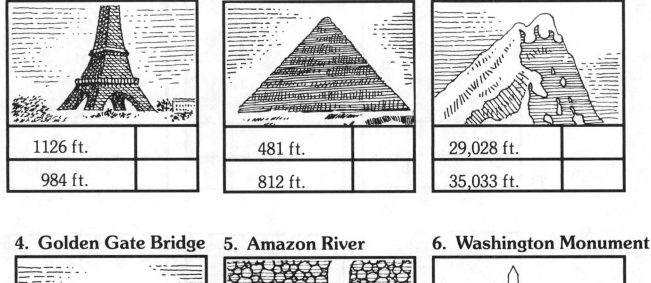

1126 ft.	
984 ft.	

2. Great Pyramid

481 ft.	
812 ft.	

3. Mt. Everest

29,028 ft.	
35,033 ft.	

4. Golden Gate Bridge

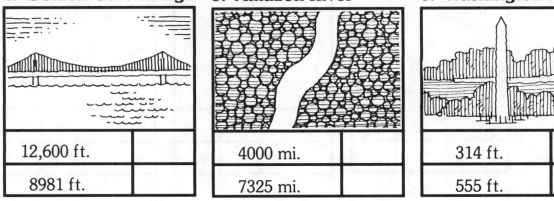

12,600 ft.	
8981 ft.	

5. Amazon River

4000 mi.	
7325 mi.	

6. Washington Monument

314 ft.	
555 ft.	

7. Niagara Falls

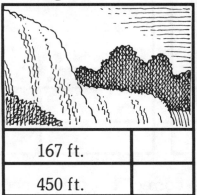

167 ft.	
450 ft.	

8. Empire State Bldg.

1472 ft.	
1245 ft.	

9. Mt. McKinley

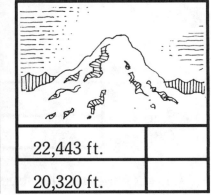

22,443 ft.	
20,320 ft.	

Pick two teammates and research the significance of one of the above "famous measurements" with them.

GA1095

Famous Measurements II
Student Work Sheet (classwork or homework)

After completing Famous Measurements I, find nine additional famous measures to challenge your classmates. Draw an illustration and include the real and made-up choice. If your classmates put their answers on another sheet, your Famous Measurements can be exchanged a number of times.

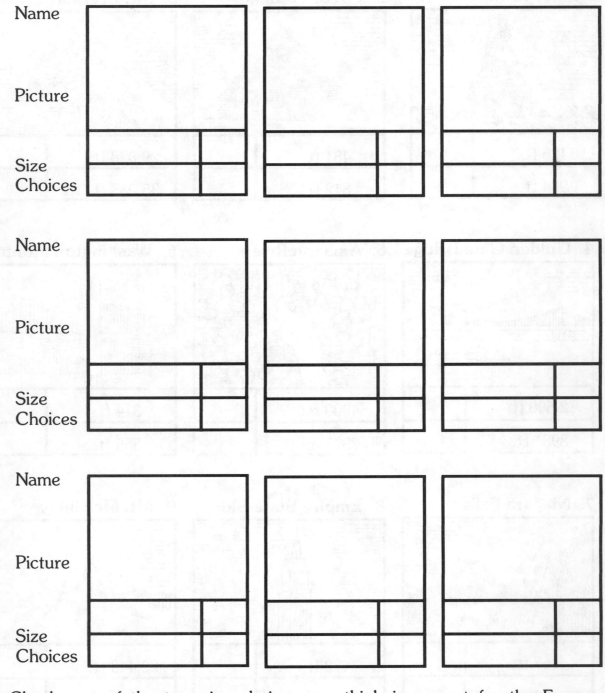

Name

Picture

Size Choices

Check one of the two size choices you think is correct for the Famous Measurements named and illustrated above. Compare scores for a winner.

GA1095

Famous Measurement Facts

I. Before starting the Famous Measurements I work sheet, try to guess the size of each of these famous figures.

	Figure	Size Guess	Actual Size	Difference
1.	Eiffel Tower			
2.	Great Pyramid			
3.	Mt. Everest			
4.	Golden Gate Bridge			
5.	Amazon River			
6.	Washington Monu.			
7.	Niagara Falls			
8.	Empire State Bldg.			
9.	Mt. McKinley			
10.	A Friend's Height			
11.	A Friend's Weight			

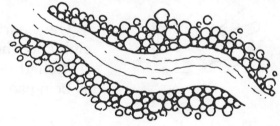

II. Illustrate two of the above figures and include significant measurement facts next to your choices.

Illustration I	Facts
Illustration II	**Facts**

GA1095

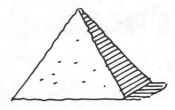

Early Measurement History

Early measurement was a conglomeration of irregular, nonstandard units. Use the following ideas to do some simple measures in your classroom. Compare your answers to your classmates'.

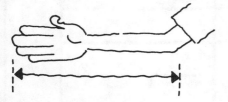

A *cubit*, used by the Egyptians to build the pyramids, is the measure from the tip of your middle finger to the tip of your elbow.

The *fathom* is the measure from fingertip to fingertip when your arms are stretched sideways as far as they go. You sometimes still see rope and thread measured this way. Rope with knots showing depth in fathoms (often dropped in the water) have been replaced by sophisticated electronic depth finders on most boats.

The *hand/span* is the measure from the tip of your pinky to the tip of your thumb when your hand is stretched out. You still hear people talk about horses as being so many hands high.

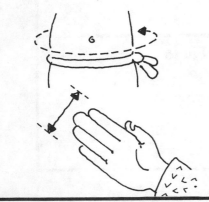

The *pace* (two steps) was said to be used by the Romans to describe the rate of movement of their soldiers.

The *girth* is the measure around your stomach (your belt measure). Fishing line was measured in girths.

The width found by placing your four fingers together is called the *palm*.

GA1095

Early Measurement History
Student Work Sheet

I. Review the measures on the Early Measurement History page. Can you discover any obscure measurement facts that you can add to the chart below? Use these "old time" measures to measure some common classroom items. *Some measures will be smaller than what was asked for, such as you wouldn't measure your desk with a pace, but if you do, this measure and others can be expressed in a fraction.

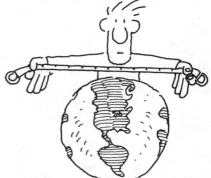

	Palm	Cubit	Pace	Fathom	Girth	Span
Desk Width			*			
Desk Length						
Room Width						
Room Length						
Your Height						
Friend's Height						
Door Width						
Door Length						
Window Width						
Window Length						
Pane Width						
Pane Length						

II. Cut your palm, span and cubit out of butcher or construction paper. Fill them with cutout pictures of things that they can measure. Mount them on a bulletin board. Include your classmates in this collage.

13

Historical Time

Each time dial represents one hundred years. Your teacher will call out famous events in history. You set your time dial to the date (correct answer). The dials can also be used with the Time Trials Student Sheet.

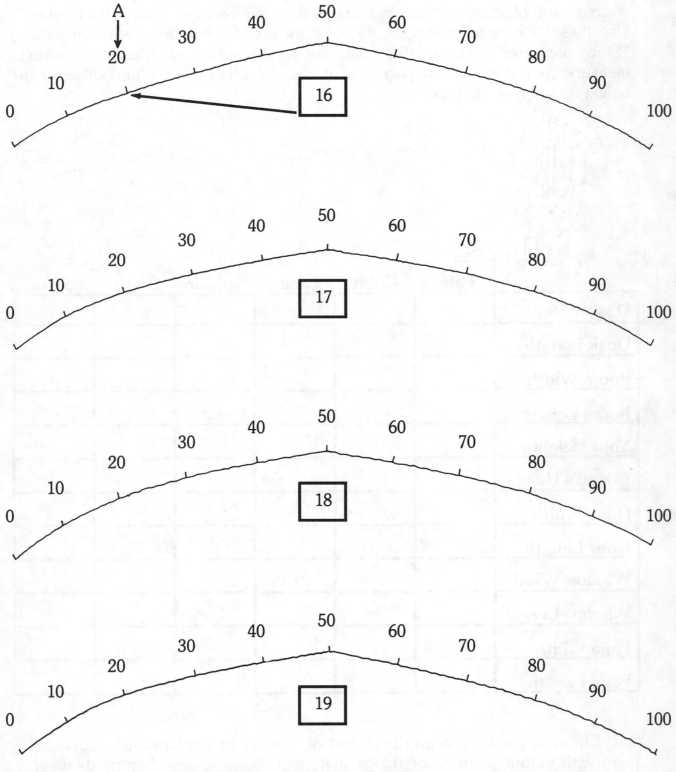

If your teacher tells you "Pilgrims settled at Plymouth Rock," place your pencil on the 16 and the point on 20 (date 1620).

GA1095

Time Trials
Student Work Sheet

Use your time dials to represent the following events. Place the events letter and an arrow A↓ on the correct dial.

Example:

A. Pilgrims settled at Plymouth Rock   1620

B. This year is _____.

C. The year you were born was _____.

D. Your favorite historical event. Please be ready to explain why the event interests you.

E. What year was your state or town founded?

F. Signing of the Declaration of Independence

G. Washington burned during this war.

H. The Wright brothers first flight at Kitty Hawk

I. Landing of man on the moon

J. United States entry into WW II (Pearl Harbor)

K. Lindbergh's first flight across the Atlantic Ocean

L. Student Choice

M. Student Choice

Record and illustrate two little known events that should be better remembered in history. How much *time* has passed since the events occurred?

Date _____ Time _____   Date _____ Time _____

The All-Purpose Clock
Teacher Directions

The blank clock faces can be used to reinforce all the time units in your curriculum or the "clock projects" suggested below.

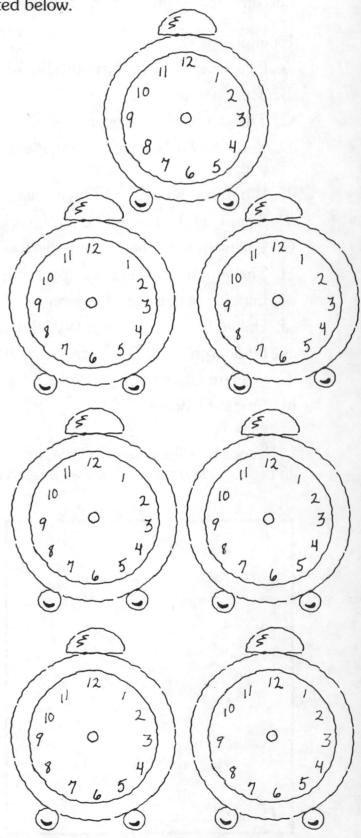

I. You show time in words (half past two) or numbers (3:15). Student draws correct clock hands.

II. After a discussion of time zones, the student has to find a location in four time zones on each side of his zone. The city and time is recorded for each.

III. An instant time diary is kept. The class decides on nine Saturday times. Students record what they were doing at that time.

IV. The student records sunset and sunrise times for the first day of summer, winter, fall and spring.

V. The students create a television guide showing the clock setting and an illustration of their favorite shows.

VI. Many historical events (first man on moon) have exact times. Illustrate and show the time for nine events. This should be a three-person team assignment.

VII. Take the clock faces and design five one-of-a-kind time devices.

VIII. Make replicas of five famous clocks. (Big Ben, William Penn in Philadelphia, etc.)

16

GA1095

Measuring Time

To find out how *long* a person lived, you subtract the year he was *born from* the year he died. To find out how *long ago* a person lived, you *subtract the date of death from* the present date.

Highlight the events in the lives of four famous people of the past. Show the computation for their ages at death and how long ago they lived.

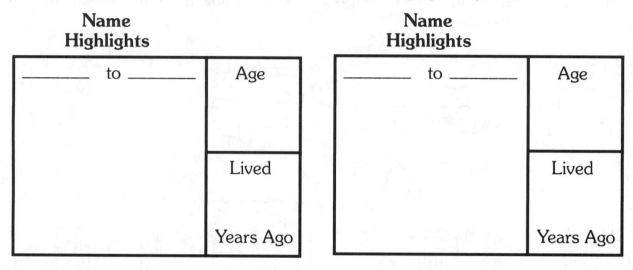

Name
Highlights

_____ to _____ | Age
| Lived
| Years Ago

Name
Highlights

_____ to _____ | Age
| Lived
| Years Ago

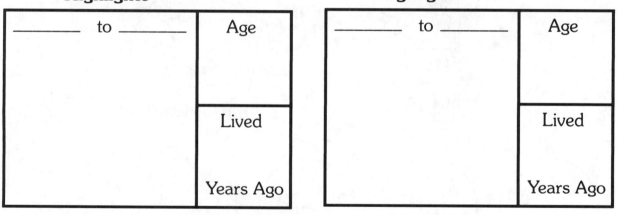

Name
Highlights

_____ to _____ | Age
| Lived
| Years Ago

Name
Highlights

_____ to _____ | Age
| Lived
| Years Ago

Teacher Hint: You may want to duplicate a list of people that relate to your mathematics curriculum.

GA1095

The Prize Is Right
Area and Circumference Prediction

Game I (Area)   **Game II (Circumference)**

Pick a competitor. The object is to predict the area or circumference of the circles below. The person with the closest prediction to circle 1 wins prize 1 and places his/her initials in the price tag. Continue the competition until all the prizes are won.

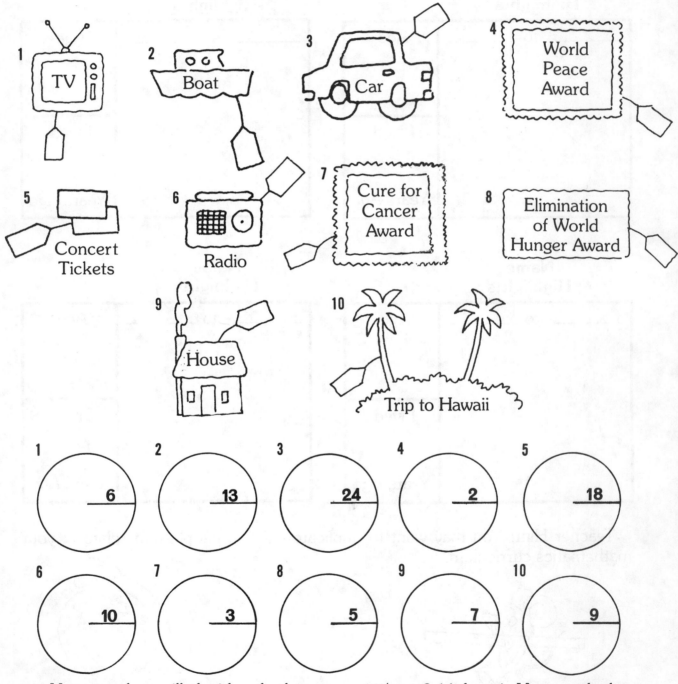

Your teacher will decide whether to use $\frac{22}{7}$ or 3.14 for pi. Use a calculator to see who is closest.

18

GA1095

The Prize Is Right
Blank Master

Take home one or more of these prizes by outpredicting your partner on the problems below. Remember to put your initials in the price tag if your guess was the closest.

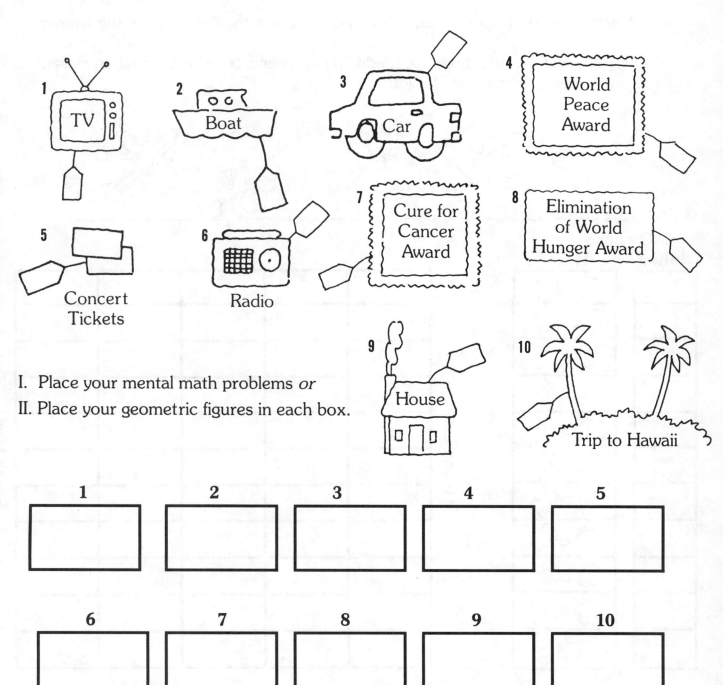

1 TV

2 Boat

3 Car

4 World Peace Award

5 Concert Tickets

6 Radio

7 Cure for Cancer Award

8 Elimination of World Hunger Award

9 House

10 Trip to Hawaii

I. Place your mental math problems *or*
II. Place your geometric figures in each box.

1	2	3	4	5

6	7	8	9	10

GA1095

Decimal Horse Race

Materials: Colored pencils or crayons; two dice each numbered $\frac{0}{10}$, $\frac{1}{10}$, $\frac{2}{10}$, $\frac{3}{10}$, $\frac{4}{10}$, $\frac{5}{10}$

Choices: Each player selects five horses below; alternate when selecting and place your initial on each horse you selected.

Object: The first player to have three horses cross the finish line is the winner.

Play: Alternate turns; throw dice; add fractions and color in decimal equivalent shown on each horse's saddlecloth.

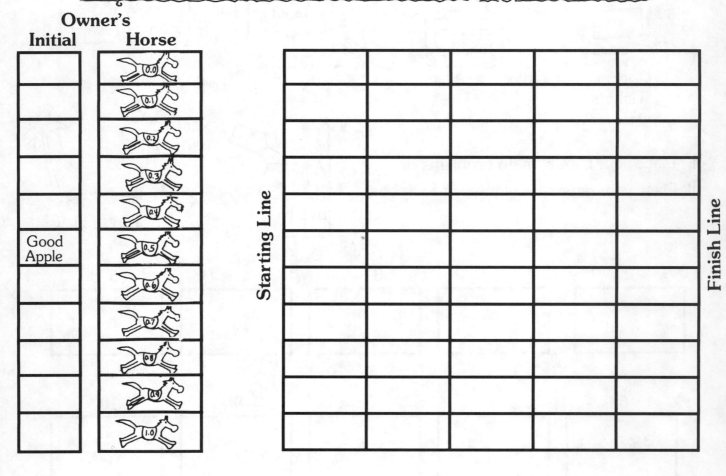

Color in the boxes from left to right after each throw is added.

GA1095

Illustrated World Times

Many banks, shopping malls and stock markets have displays of clocks with cities' names under them. The clocks show a comparison of what time it is here and what time it is in the cities represented by the clocks. This technique could be more creative if a scene depicting that city or country were displayed. Pick four locations throughout the United States or world. Give their present time and a drawing depicting that area. Complete this activity on 11" x 14" paper.

Present time here _____

Area _____

Area _____

Area _____

Area _____

GA1095

Measuring Humor
The Joke of the Day

Your teacher will be reading six jokes to you. You are to rate each joke on the humor index below. Each column has ten boxes for you to graph your feelings about each joke on a scale of one to ten. After you complete your graph, answer the questions below.

Joke Graph

1	2	A	3	4	B	5	6

1. Which joke did you rate the highest? _____

2. Which joke received your lowest rating? _____

3. What was the difference between your high and low ratings? _____

4. What was your average for the six jokes (total score divided by six)? _____

5. Use columns A and B to rate two of your classmates' jokes.

Teacher Hint: You can use your own jokes or the jokes on the next page.

GA1095

Measuring Decibels

Sound in some instances is measured in decibels. You have been provided with twelve decibel meters and twelve jokes. You will read the joke to a subject and record his visible response to the joke or ask him to rate the creativeness (1-10) of each offering. Draw a needle on each meter to show the subject's decibel response.

A. What do apples use to travel from planet to planet?   (an applesaucer)
B. What was the world's first apple called?   (Adam's apple)
C. What is large, red and goes bam, bam, bam, bam?   (a four-door apple)
D. What is red, dangerous and hangs in a tree?   (an apple with a machine gun)
E. How do you divide 9 apples among 11 people?   (make applesauce)
F. What kind of apples does McDonald's serve?   (Macintosh)
G. What is the favorite dessert of mathematicians?   (apple pie [pi])
H. A person pro apple is called?   (an apple cider [sider])
I. What is the bad part of Appletown called?   (The Pits)
J. What part of the service protects apples?   The Apple Core [Corps])
K. What is a bathroom called in Appleseed Junction?   (a Johnny)
L. What do judges look for in an apple judging contest?   (appeal [a peel])

Draw in the needle to show the reaction to each joke above.

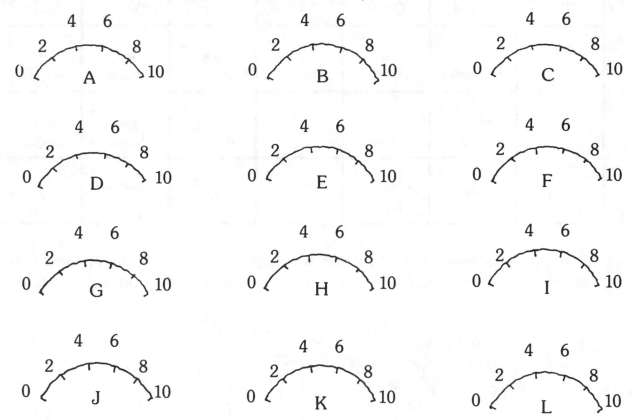

What was the total amount of reaction generated?

GA1095

Measure Match
Student Work Sheet

Materials: One number cube (1, 2, 3, 4, 5, 6)

Object: Throw cube; look in right-hand corner for number thrown; match answer with another equivalent answer somewhere else on the board; color in both answers. If you throw a number (as game winds down) that doesn't appear in any corner, you lose your turn.

1 Leap Year	**2** 16 Ounces	**3** 5280 Feet	**4** 12 Dozen	**5** 3 Feet	**6** 100 Years	**1** ⁹⁄₁₀ of a Mile
2 168 Hours	**3** 13	**4** 2 Cups	**5** A Minute	**6** A Year	**1** 3600 Seconds	**2** 4 Quarts
3 186,200 Miles Per/Sec.	**4** A Gross	**5** Speed of Sound	**6** A Century	**1** A Ton	**2** Ten	**3** A Foot
4 An Hour	**5** A Score	**6** A Quart		**1** 20 Years	**2** A Yard	**3** A Meter
4 Perfect in Gymnastics	**5** A Kilometer	**6** A Week	**1** 2000 Pounds	**2** 39.4 Inches	**3** A Gallon	**4** 60 Seconds
5 12 Inches	**6** A Pint	**1** ½ Mile	**2** 1100 Feet Per Second	**3** A Pound	**4** 880 Yards	**5** 1000 Years
6 Baker's Dozen	**1** A Millennium	**2** 366 Days	**3** 12 Months	**4** A Mile	**5** Speed of Light	**6** 2 Pints

Scoring: Last one to color in a match wins; alternate turns. Blank sheet follows so you can design your own game. Record your matches on a separate sheet of paper.

We're playing LEAP YEAR!

LEAP YEAR

Measure Match
Blank Master

Review the rules of Measure Match on the preceding page. Pick a mathematical/ measurement theme of your own and enter the pairs of choices in the chart below. Give the completed sheet to two competitors. How about shapes and their formulas? Have you considered mathematicians and their discoveries?

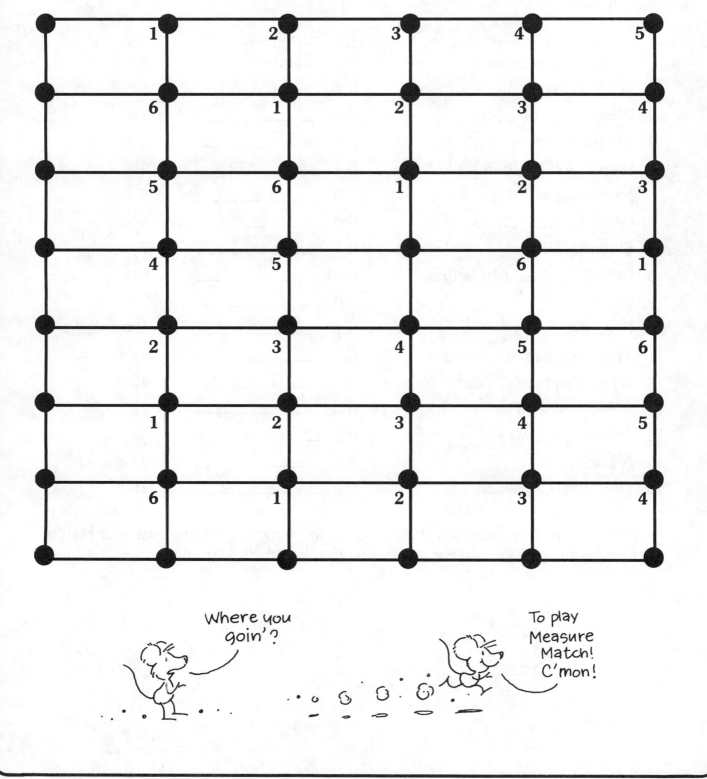

GA1095

Rollover
Love and Hate Measurement Graphs

Love or Hate can be found in each answer below. In some answers the letters are consecutive. In other answers the letters are in word order but may have additional letters spaced between the L-O-V-E or H-A-T-E. Clues will help you find each answer. Multiply the problem number times the letters in your answer for your score.

Clue	Hint	Answer	Score
Example: Car Warmer	(H)	**Heater**	$1 \times 6 = 6$
1. Type of Sweater	(L)	_____	$1 \times$
2. Window Hit by a Rock	(H)	_____	$2 \times$
3. Winter Handwarmer	(L)	_____	$3 \times$
4. French Art Museum	(L)	_____	$4 \times$
5. Movie House	(H)	_____	$5 \times$
6. "Wonderland" Character	(H)	_____	$6 \times$
7. Sloppily Dressed	(L)	_____	$7 \times$
8. Book _____, *Macbeth and Me*	(H)	_____	$8 \times$
9. Idle Talk	(H)	_____	$9 \times$
10. Beautiful	(L)	_____	$10 \times$
11. The Breakfast of Champions	(H)	_____	$11 \times$
12. A Door with Shade-like Windows	(L)	_____	$12 \times$
13. A Section of a Book	(H)	_____	$13 \times$
14. To Promise Harm	(H)	_____	$14 \times$
15. A Lucky Leaf	(L)	_____	$15 \times$
16. One Who Copies on Tests	(H)	_____	$16 \times$

After completing this work sheet, use the following page to present your results in four forms: pictograph, bar graph, line graph and circle graph.

GA1095

You Are Measured by Your Graphs

Student Work Sheet

Graphs that are full of meaning, attractive and creative can be the keystone to the success of your presentations, projects and research. Most are variations of picture, line, bar or circle graphs.

A. Review these four types of graphs with your classmates.
B. Make a mini booklet of the most original graphs found in newspapers, books and magazines.
C. Investigate how computers have enhanced graph making and the graphic presentation of ideas.
D. Use this knowledge to create four graphs that will represent the preceding Love and Hate activity or a new topic you or your teacher suggested/researched/surveyed.
E. Use the space below to plan before enlarging your ideas.

Line	Bar
Picture	**Circle**

GA1095

Metric Words

All words that have exactly ten letters are called "metric words." The clues given below will help you find "metric words." You are then asked to evaluate the following types of letters in your word and express them as a decimal and then as a percent. V means compute the vowels; C means compute the consonants; S means compute the straight letters.

Clue	Answer	V	C	S
Example: A Bird	WOODPECKER	.4	.6	.4
1. A U.S. State	_____	__	__	__
2. A Country	_____	__	__	__
3. A Boy's Name	_____	__	__	__
*4. A Girl's Name	_____	__	__	__
5. A U.S. City	_____	__	__	__
6. A Travel Vehicle	_____	__	__	__
*7. A Character from History	_____	__	__	__
8. Lincoln and Washington	_____	__	__	__
9. Daily News and Inquirer	_____	__	__	__
*10. The Earth's Spin Around Sun	_____	__	__	__
*11. A Sport	_____	__	__	__
*12. Room Temperature Regulator	_____	__	__	__

Can you find a "metric word" that is

a. 20% vowels? _____

b. 30% vowels? _____

c. 40% vowels? _____

d. 50% vowels? _____

Students: Print your answers in uppercase letters. Straight letters contain only straight lines.

GA1095

Multiply Then Order
Drill for Area of Rectangle
Student Work Sheet

Complete each problem. Place your words in size order from smallest to largest. Record the secret sentence below.

1.

Problem	Answer	Word
2 × 9		SEEM
3 × 5		FAR
9 × 3		WELL
5 × 4		TO
2 × 6		SO
8 × 3		DOING
4 × 4		YOU
11 × 2		BE

2.

Problem	Answer	Word
9 × 5		PROBLEMS
8 × 8		DO
13 × 4		HARDER
8 × 6		ARE
6 × 9		TO
6 × 6		YES
10 × 5		GETTING
3 × 14		THESE

3.

Problem	Answer	Word
3 × 30		HAVING
49 × 2		TROUBLE
9 × 9		ARE
8 × 13		ANSWERS
6 × 16		ANY
11 × 8		YOU
4 × 25		WITH
17 × 6		YOUR

4.

Problem	Answer	Word
8 × 2		THE
4 × 6		SAVED
3 × 4		WAS
4 × 8		END
7 × 4		THE
6 × 3		EASIEST
5 × 5		FOR
10 × 2		ONE

Sentences:

1. ___ ___ ___ ___ ___ ___ ___ ___
2. ___ ___ ___ ___ ___ ___ ___ ___
3. ___ ___ ___ ___ ___ ___ ___ ___
4. ___ ___ ___ ___ ___ ___ ___ ___

GA1095

Multiply Then Order

Blank Master

Design your own Multiply Then Order activity. Complete the problems below to find each word's value. Order your words from smallest to largest in the blanks below. You will then have the secret sentence for each group of problems. Try to multiply decimals or fractions for your selection.

1.

Problem	Answer	Word

2.

Problem	Answer	Word

3.

Problem	Answer	Word

4.

Problem	Answer	Word

Sentences:

1. _____ _____ _____ _____ _____ _____ _____

2. _____ _____ _____ _____ _____ _____ _____

3. _____ _____ _____ _____ _____ _____ _____

4. _____ _____ _____ _____ _____ _____ _____

GA1095

Measuring Fractions of an Inch

There are many items that are less than an inch wide (paper clips, coins, erasers, etc.). The fractional rulers below have the ability to measure those items and others of your own choosing.

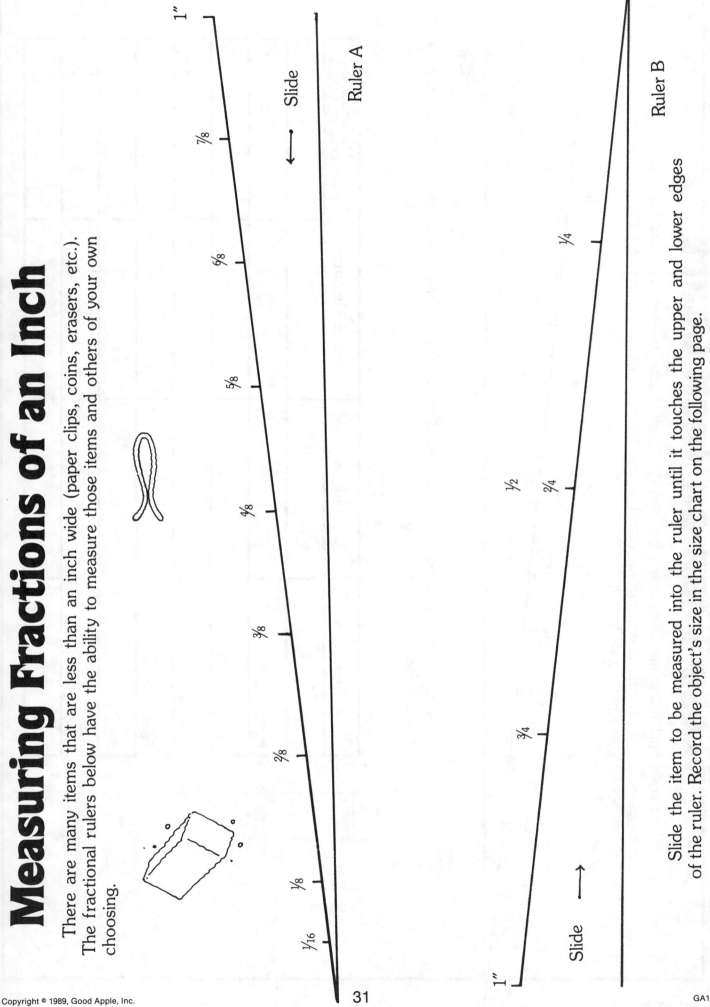

Slide the item to be measured into the ruler until it touches the upper and lower edges of the ruler. Record the object's size in the size chart on the following page.

31

GA1095

Less-Than-an-Inch Chart

This fractional ruler measures items less than an inch. Slide the item into the ruler until it touches the upper and lower edges. Record your answers in the chart below. Make a good guess before you measure each item.

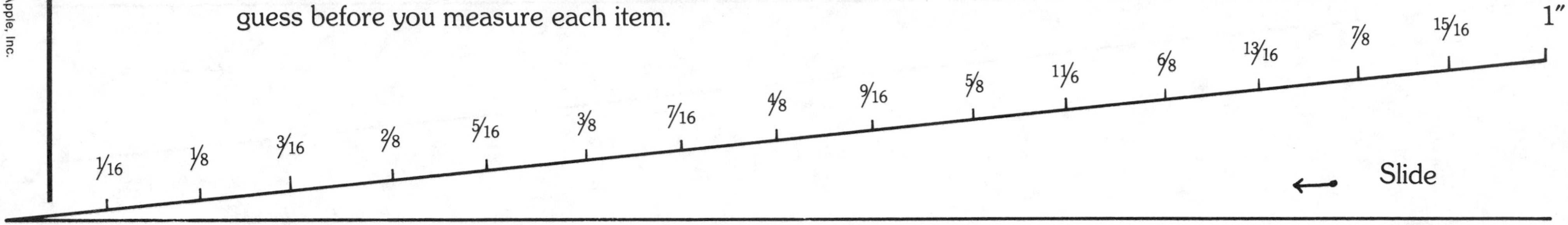

Ruler markings: 1/16 3/16 2/8 5/16 3/8 7/16 4/8 9/16 5/8 11/16 6/8 13/16 7/8 15/16 1"

← Slide

Ruler C

This chart can be used with rulers A, B or C. Explain the difference in each ruler. How can we make ruler C even more exact?

Item	Guess	Actual Measure	Difference (Show Problem)
Dime			
Penny			
Nickel			
Example: Quarter	12/16	15/16	15/16 − 12/16 = 3/16
Paper Clip			
Pencil			
Choice			
Choice			

GA1095

The Decimal Ruler

After you have worked with the fractional ruler activities, you might find the decimal challenge a little harder to solve.

What part of an inch will these measure?

A. Penny _____   B. Nickel _____   C. Dime _____   D. Quarter _____

E. Can you find four objects that will total 1 inch?

_____   _____

F. What object comes closest to half an inch? quarter?

_____   _____

G. How many four-letter words can you find that will equal 1 inch? Can you find four?

_____   _____

H. How long are the first three letters of your name?

_____   _____

I. What is the longest and shortest three-letter name you can find?

(S) _____   (L) _____

Use this ruler to complete this page and the activities on the following pages.

How long are the first 3 letters in your name?

GA1095

Words Worth an Inch

I. Use the hundredths of an inch ruler to determine the values for each of these letters.

Example: A = .05 or 5/100   H = .40 or 40/100

       L =   D =   J =

       R =   P =   E =

II. Use the letter values on the hundredths ruler to determine each word's total value.

Example: PAT = .80 + .05 + .10 = .95

       L =   B =   G =   H=

       O =   E =   O =   A=

       V =   S =   L =   R=

       E = _____   T = _____   F = _____   D=_____

III. The word PAST (.80 + .05 + .05 + .10) and SARA (.05 + .05 + .85 + .05) are *one-inch* words. How many *one-inch* words can you and your classmates add to these?

1. _____   6. _____
2. _____   7. _____
3. _____   8. _____
4. _____   9. _____
5. _____   10. _____

IV. What is the smallest valued antonym, synonym and homonym that you can find?

1. antonym   _____ + _____ = _____ + _____ =
2. synonym   _____ + _____ = _____ + _____ =
3. homonym   _____ + _____ = _____ + _____ =

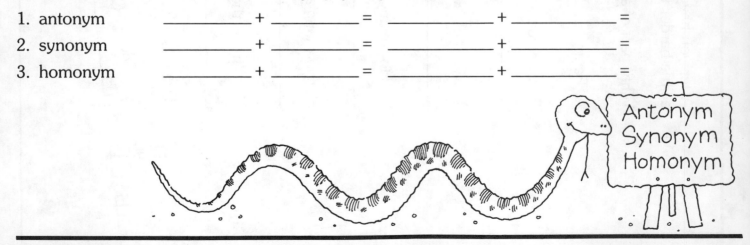

Antonym
Synonym
Homonym

GA1095

Decimal Ruler Chart

Use your decimal ruler letters to complete the chart below. Find the largest and smallest valued word in each category. Answers will vary, so enter into friendly competition with your classmates. Work in teams of four and enter your team's best answer.

	Smallest Value	Total	Largest Value	Total
2-letter word	AS = .05 + .05	.10	OR = .75 + .85	1.60
3-letter word				
4-letter word				
5-letter word				
6-letter word				
A color				
A fruit				
*First name				
*Last name				
A vegetable				
A game				
A sport				
A drink				

* Must be a member of your team

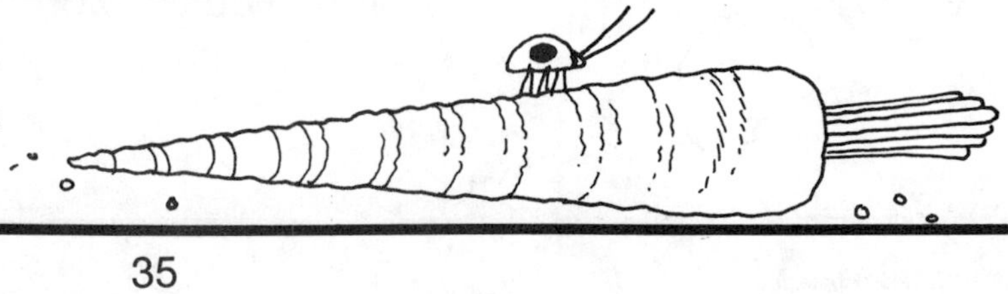

GA1095

Measure-Your-Stroke Golf Course

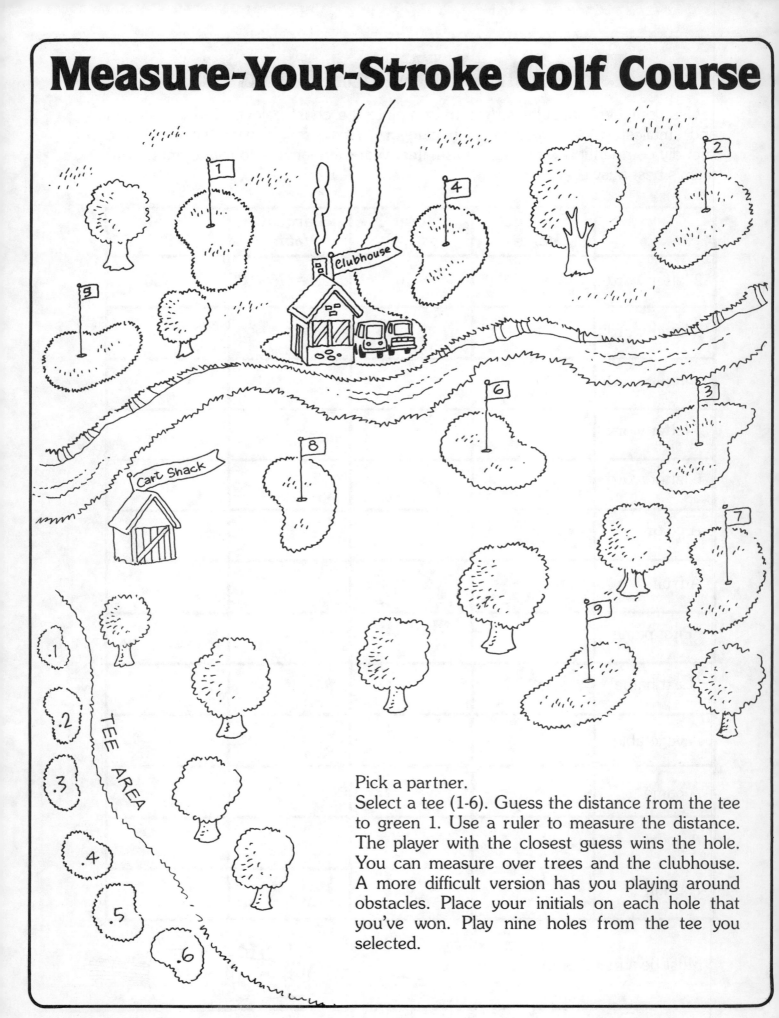

Pick a partner.
Select a tee (1-6). Guess the distance from the tee to green 1. Use a ruler to measure the distance. The player with the closest guess wins the hole. You can measure over trees and the clubhouse. A more difficult version has you playing around obstacles. Place your initials on each hole that you've won. Play nine holes from the tee you selected.

GA1095

Measure Your Golf Stroke
Student/Teacher Directions

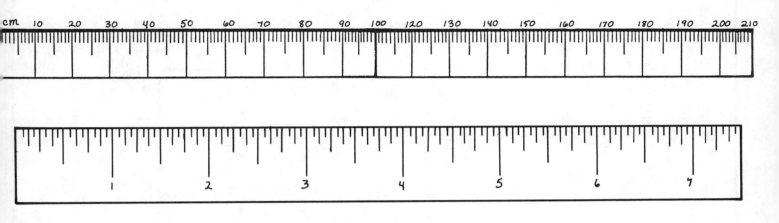

There are six tee-off areas on the nine-hole golf course work sheet. Roll a cube or pick a number to decide what tee will be used for the first round. Look at the distance from the tee selected to the first green. Each player now records his guess from tee to the bottom of the flag on hole 1 (point to point). The closest guess wins that hole. You can play nine or eighteen holes. Fifty-four holes are available (six tees x nine greens). Centimeter and eighth-inch rulers are available. Your teacher may want you to select another smaller or larger standard of measure. Use the scorecard to record your progress and victories.

Scorecard

Hole	Guess Player A	Guess Player B	Actual Distance	Winner's Initials
1				
2				
3				
4				
5				
6				
7				
8				
9				

GA1095

Meter War

This game can be played on a regular meterstick marked off in centimeters or on the gameboard replica below. Cut out the tank and place it on the 50-centimeter location on the meterstick. Roll two dice to see who goes first. That player rolls two dice and multiplies. The answer will tell you how many centimeters to move toward that person's town. The next player throws, multiplies and tries to move the tank back toward the opponent's town. First player to land on the town wins the game. Capturing the town twice wins the war.

Cut out tank.
Place pointer on 50 cm.

Meterstick

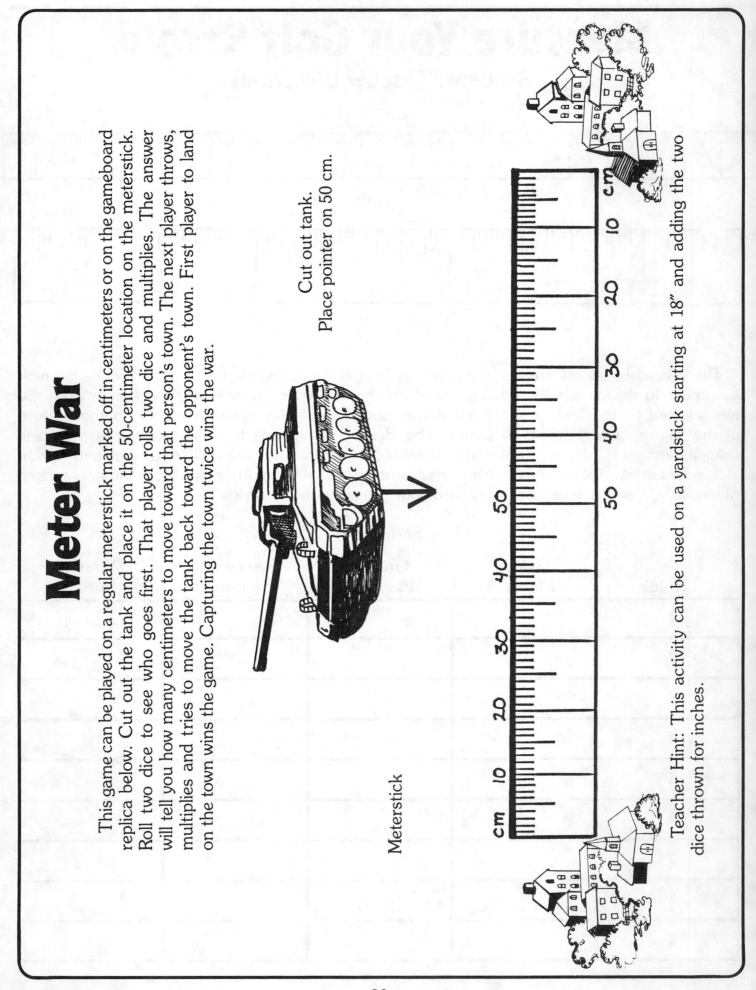

Teacher Hint: This activity can be used on a yardstick starting at 18" and adding the two dice thrown for inches.

GA1095

The All-Purpose Area and Volume

Gameboard

The rule for today is: formula _____

I. There are two teams with one color crayon for each team.

II. Roll two or three number cubes depending on the formula for today.

III. Find and color in the result.

IV. The first one to play the third color in any column or row is the winner.

V. Cubes are numbered 1-6.

1	2	3	4	5	6	7	8
9	10	11	12	13	14	15	16
17	18	19	20	21	22	23	24
25	26	27	28	29	30	31	32
33	34	35	36	37	38	39	40
41	42	44	45	48	50	54	55
60	64	66	72	75	80	90	96
100	108	120	125	144	150	180	216

Teacher Hint: This gameboard works best for area of a rectangle (2 cubes); volume of a cube (3 cubes); area of a triangle (2 cubes); halves roundup (4 ½ = 5); area of a trapezoid (3 cubes).

GA1095

Monopolize Your Perimeter

Gameboard

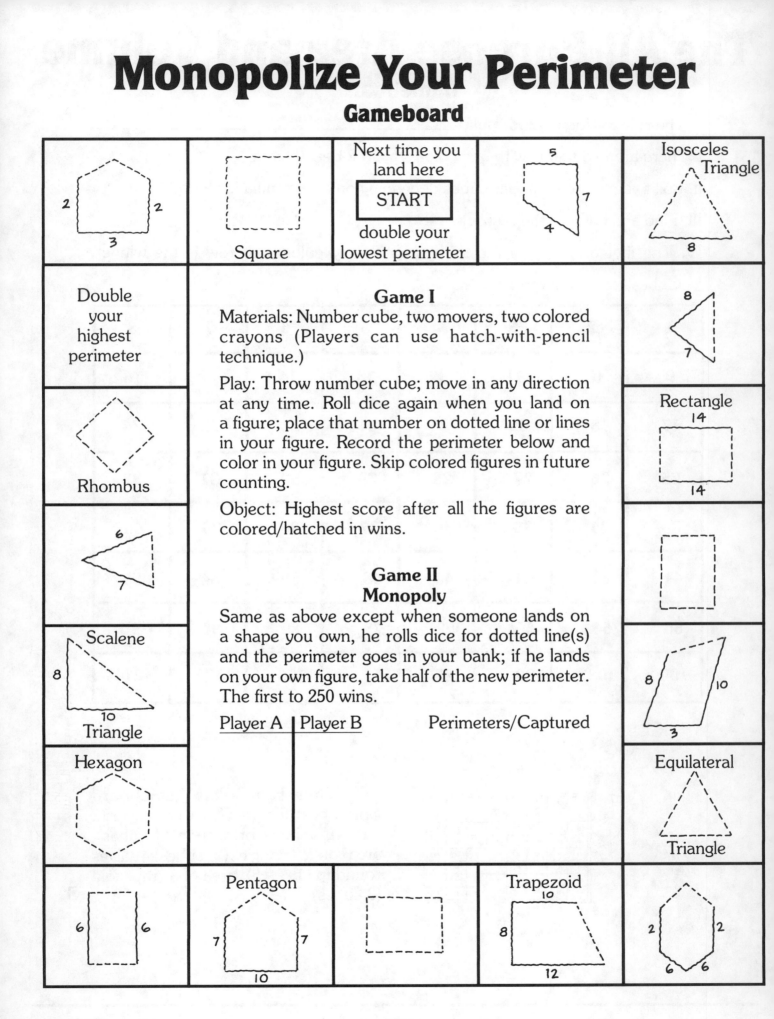

2
2
3
Square
Next time you land here
START
double your lowest perimeter
5
7
4
Isosceles Triangle
8

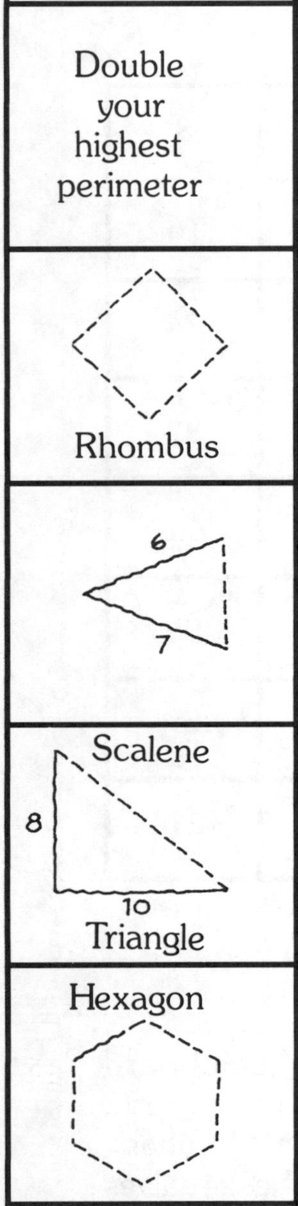
Double your highest perimeter
Rhombus
6
7
Scalene
8
10
Triangle
Hexagon

Game I

Materials: Number cube, two movers, two colored crayons (Players can use hatch-with-pencil technique.)

Play: Throw number cube; move in any direction at any time. Roll dice again when you land on a figure; place that number on dotted line or lines in your figure. Record the perimeter below and color in your figure. Skip colored figures in future counting.

Object: Highest score after all the figures are colored/hatched in wins.

Game II
Monopoly

Same as above except when someone lands on a shape you own, he rolls dice for dotted line(s) and the perimeter goes in your bank; if he lands on your own figure, take half of the new perimeter. The first to 250 wins.

Player A	Player B	Perimeters/Captured

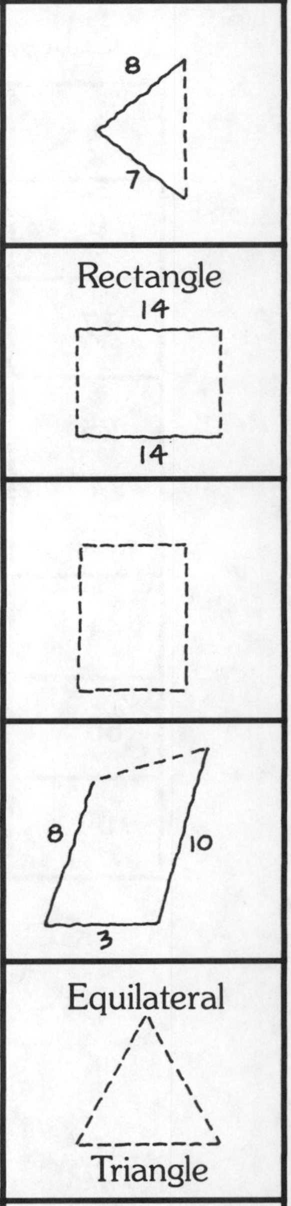
8
7
Rectangle
14
14
8
10
3
Equilateral
Triangle

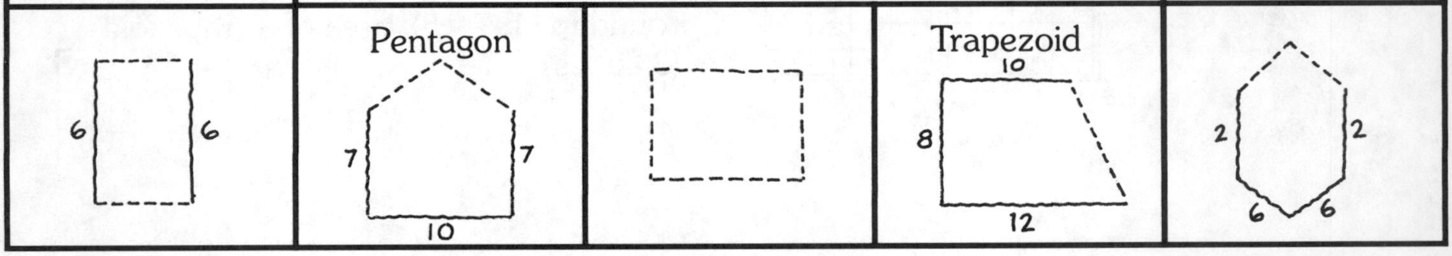
6
6
Pentagon
7
7
10
Trapezoid
10
8
12
2
2
6
6

Area and Perimeter of a Square
Gameboard

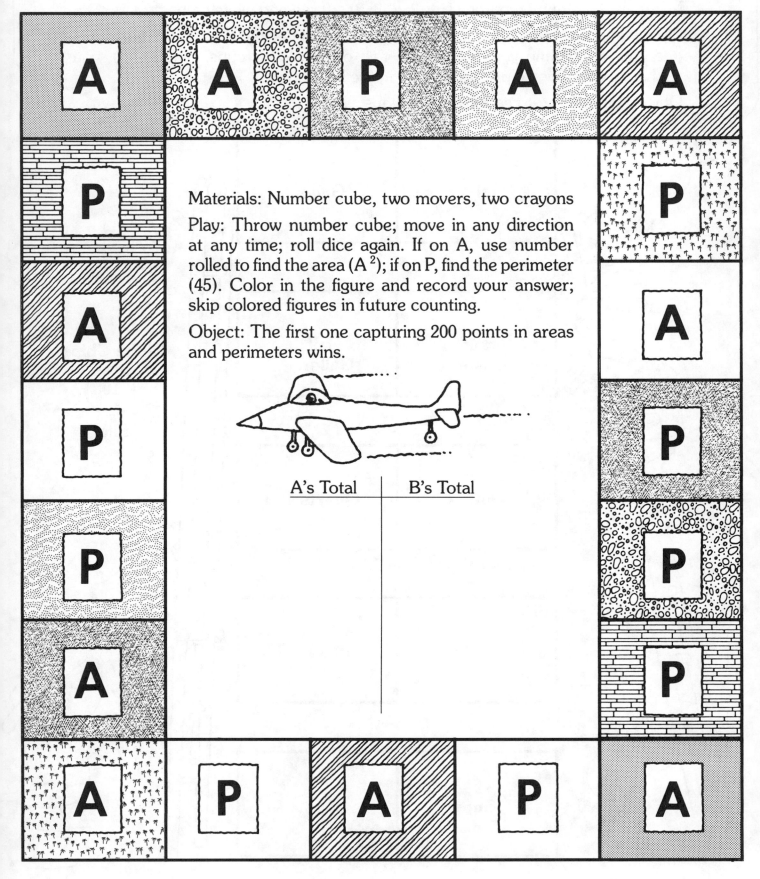

Materials: Number cube, two movers, two crayons

Play: Throw number cube; move in any direction at any time; roll dice again. If on A, use number rolled to find the area (A²); if on P, find the perimeter (45). Color in the figure and record your answer; skip colored figures in future counting.

Object: The first one capturing 200 points in areas and perimeters wins.

A's Total   B's Total

41

GA1095

Move Up to Liquid Measure
Gameboard

Materials: One number cube (1, 1, 2, 2, 3, 3), 20 red and white chips

Play: Players alternate turns throwing number cube. Each number represents one cup. Each time you accumulate two of one level (cups, pints, etc.), you exchange your two chips for one item in the level above.

Object: First player to capture two gallons wins.

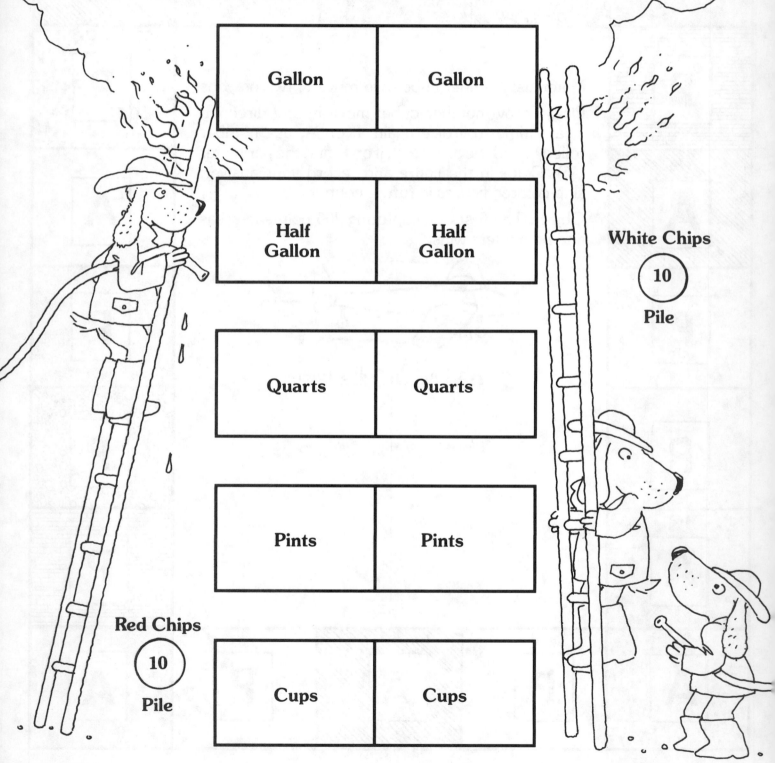

Gallon	Gallon
Half Gallon	Half Gallon
Quarts	Quarts
Pints	Pints
Cups	Cups

White Chips
10 Pile

Red Chips
10 Pile

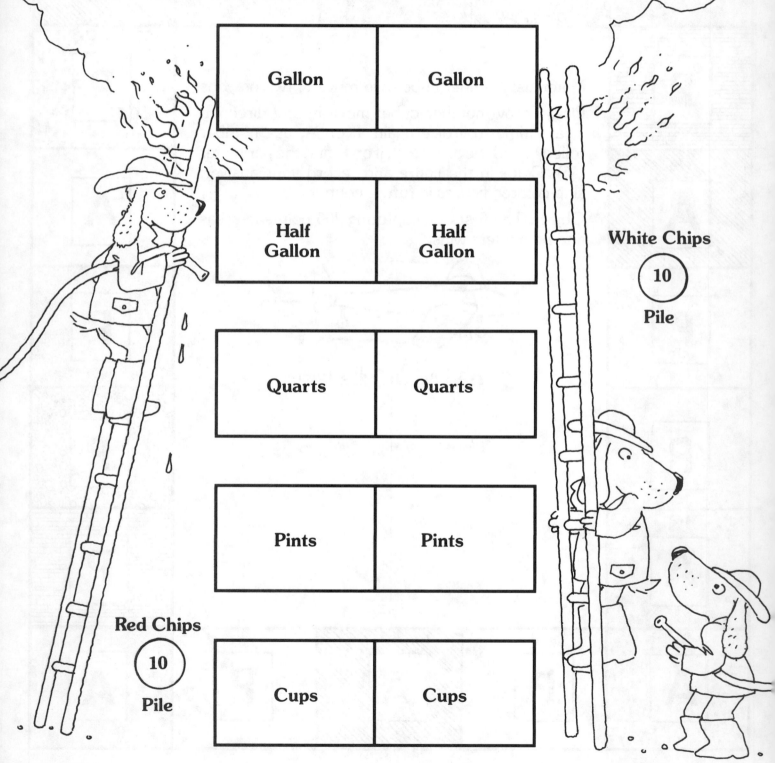

GA1095

Revolutions Per Minute

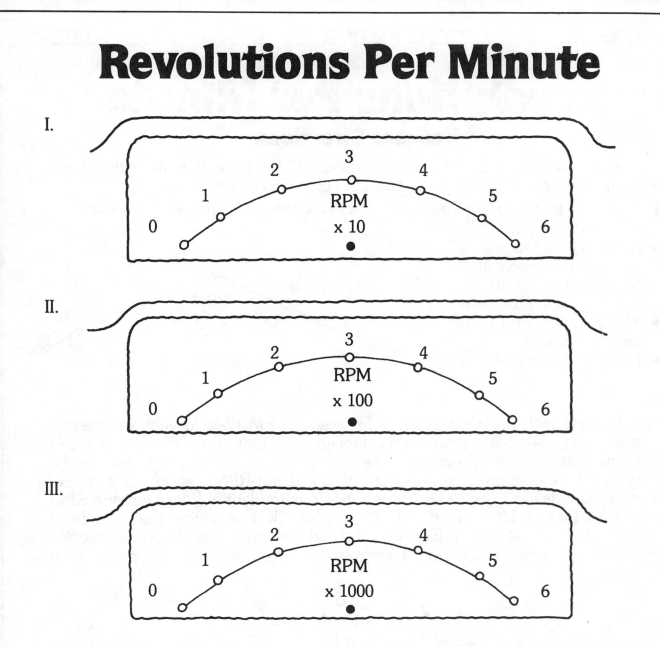

I.

II.

III.

RPM x 10

RPM x 100

RPM x 1000

Your teacher will call out various numbers (5, 15, 250, 500, 3000). Cut out your indicator needles and place them on the dial that corresponds to the numbers you hear.

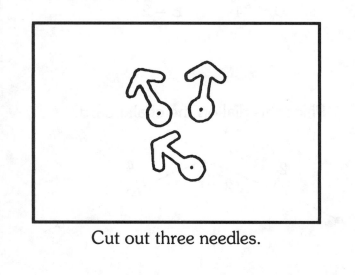

Cut out three needles.

43

GA1095

Revolutions Per Minute

Teacher Directions

The dial work sheets (meters, yards and RPM's) provide reinforcement for many measurement and mathematical concepts. They include:

- Exchange techniques in regular system of measure
- Exchange techniques in irregular systems of measure
- Multiplication of 10, 100, 1000 times a whole number
- Multiplication of 10, 100, 1000 times a decimal
- Reading charts and graphs

Place this dial on the chalkboard.

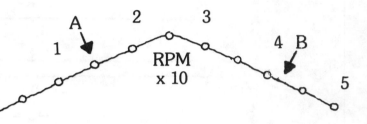

Discuss with the class reasons for having RPM dials in vehicles (insures optimum engine performance at certain speeds). Review ten times each whole number in the dial. Direct the classes' attention to the arrow $\overset{A}{\downarrow}$. Ask for the value of its location. It is not 1 ½ but 1.5. If the RPM needle points there, it would indicate 1.5 x 10 or 15. Ask the class to identify $\overset{B}{\downarrow}$ location and RPM answer (about 4.2 x 10 or 42). The author likes removing the x 10 from the dial. Then call out problems 6 x 7 = and have the class place their needles on the approximate location. Later a work sheet can be prepared showing dial I

I.

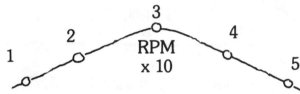

and asking students to place these letters above the following positions:

A = 5   B = 27   C = 50   D = 34   E = 2

Most cars' RPM dials are x 1000 and should idle around 500 RPM's. Ask the class to find this location on the dial. Similar identification of letters-placed-over-the-dial activities should be completed on both remaining dials (x 100 or x 1000).

Place this dial on the chalkboard.

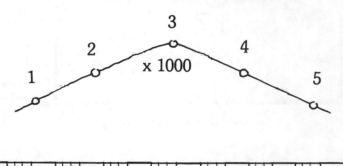

GA1095

Metric Meter Readers
Student Work Sheet

Cut out needles.

Meters

Decimeters

Centimeters

The dials show that 584 centimeters equal 5 meters, 8 decimeters and 4 centimeters. Cover the indicators and set dials to measures your teacher will call out. "What does 67 decimeters equal?" etc.

GA1095

Metric Meter Reader/Jumps

Student Work Sheet

Use your meter reader dials or jumps gameboard to complete each of the answers below.

I. What does this equal?

Example: A. 103 centimeters = __1__ meter __0__ decimeters __3__ centimeters

B. 212 centimeters = _____ meters _____ decimeters _____ centimeters

C. 47 decimeters = _____ meters _____ decimeters _____ centimeters

D. 84 decimeters = _____ meters _____ decimeters _____ centimeters

E. 400 centimeters = _____ meters _____ decimeters _____ centimeters

F. 80 centimeters = _____ meters _____ decimeters _____ centimeters

G. 12 centimeters = _____ meters _____ decimeters _____ centimeters

H. 74 centimeters = _____ meters _____ decimeters _____ centimeters

I. 155 centimeters = _____ meters _____ decimeters _____ centimeters

II. Represent each of these measures in centimeters.

Example: A. __6__ meters __0__ decimeters __3__ centimeters = __603__ centimeters

B. __73__ meters __0__ decimeters __1__ centimeter = _____ centimeters

C. __10__ meters __22__ decimeters __0__ centimeters = _____ centimeters

D. __1__ meter __31__ decimeters __2__ centimeters = _____ centimeters

E. __16__ meters __16__ decimeters __16__ centimeters = _____ centimeters

F. __22__ meters __23__ decimeters __24__ centimeters = _____ centimeters

III. Design an activity that will incorporate the use of the meter dials or jumps gameboard. Place your ideas on the back of this page.

GA1095

Yard Measure Meter Readers
Student Work Sheet

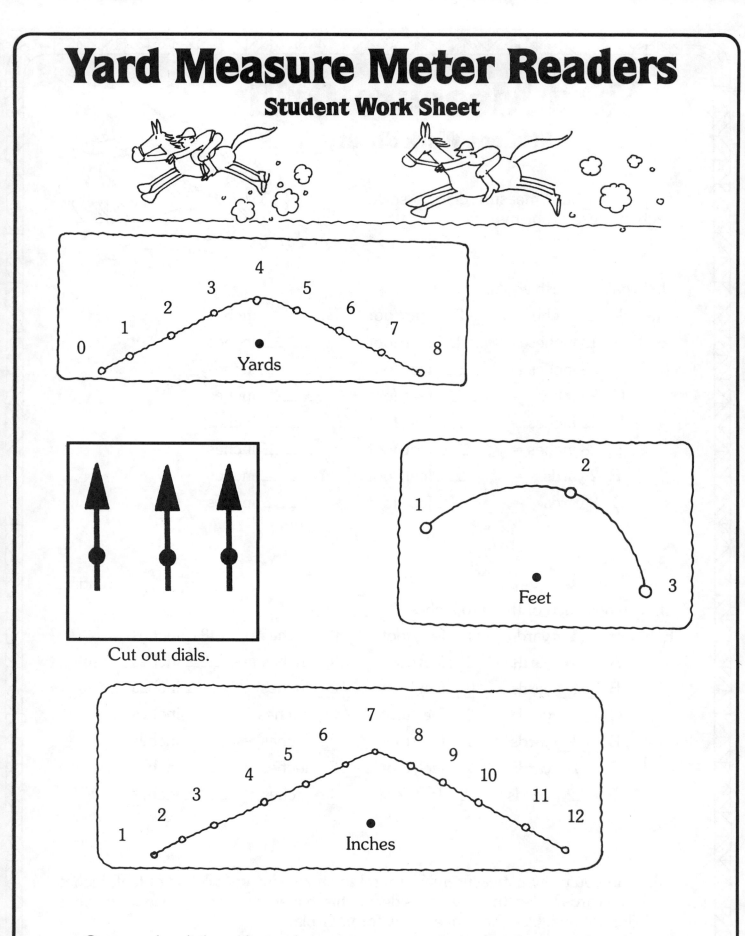

Cut out dials.

Cut out the dials and use them to represent measures your teacher dictates to you. "What does 50 inches equal?" etc.

47

GA1095

Yard Measure Drill
Student Work Sheet

Use your yard measure dials to solve each of these problems.

I. What do these equal?

Example: 26 inches = __2__ feet/foot __2__ inches

A. 13 inches = _____ feet/foot _____ inches

B. 35 inches = _____ feet/foot _____ inches

C. 9 inches = _____ feet/foot _____ inches

D. 12 inches = _____ feet/foot _____ inches

E. 28 inches = _____ feet/foot _____ inches

F. 2 yards = _____ feet/foot _____ inches

G. 8 yards = _____ feet/foot _____ inches

II. Change each of these to inches.

Example: __1__ yard __1__ feet/foot __0__ inches = __48__ inches

A. __3__ yards __3__ feet/foot __3__ inches = _____ inches

B. __4__ yards __0__ feet/foot __2__ inches = _____ inches

C. __1__ yard __2__ feet/foot __11__ inches = _____ inches

D. __8__ yards __1__ feet/foot __2__ inches = _____ inches

E. __7__ yards __7__ feet/foot __7__ inches = _____ inches

F. __12__ yards __12__ feet/foot __9__ inches = _____ inches

III. Can you draw a measurement mural to show your knowledge of feet, inches and yards? Use the reverse side of this paper or drawing paper for your illustrations. Use the space below for your plans.

GA1095

Metric Meter/Yard Reader
Teacher Directions

Place the following meters on the chalkboard/work sheet.

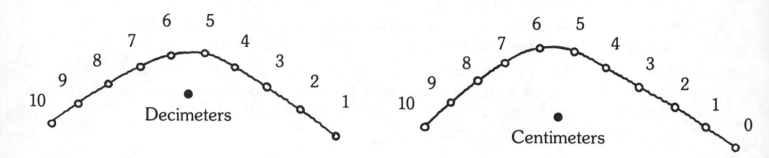

I. Have students copy meters on their papers. Using their pencils as dials, have them locate measures that you call out (remember to place a student at the chalkboard, using your drawn dials and a pointer). Teacher Hint: You could start with millimeters and centimeters.

II. Ask class to help you count out twelve centimeters. Count out first ten and ask class to explain what happens to the dials (10 centimeters becomes 1 decimeter and the centimeter dial returns to zero). Then you begin counting centimeters again, 11 = 1 decimeter and 1 centimeter, etc. Show how this technique would work for 33 centimeters, 62 centimeters, etc.

III. Add the meter to your drawing above.

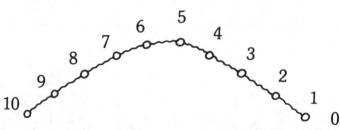

Show your students how decimeters change to meters. Give them practice with all three before doing the student work sheet.

IV. Show class the contrast with inches-to-feet-to-yards conversions.

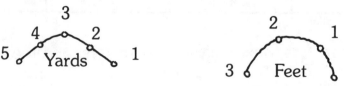
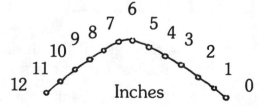

GA1095

Metric Meter Jumps
Gameboard

Players: Two teams alternating turns

Materials: A pair of number cubes (1, 2, 3, 4, 5, 6 for primary) or (1, 2, 3, 4, 5, 6 and 7, 8, 9, 10, 11, 12 for intermediate). Each team with a set of three matching movers (pieces of paper with x's and o's will suffice).

Rules: Throw two number cubes and add (primary) or multiply (intermediate) their values. Move markers to represent the sum or product. One marker at first, three as game progresses. Each number is one centimeter.

Object: First to accumulate 3 meters wins.

Super Game: Roll three cubes; place value notation; 10 meters wins.

Meters

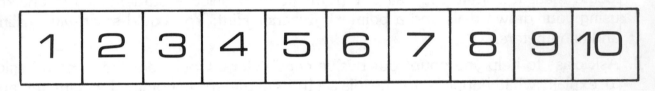

Decimeters

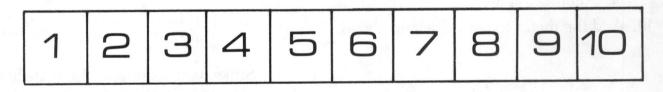

Centimeters

The smallest of the three cubes is meters, next smallest decimeters, and the next smallest centimeters.

Student Hint: Each time you accumulate 10 centimeters you move 1 decimeter. Each time you accumulate 10 decimeters, you move your marker to the next meter.

Teacher Hint: Remind students to move centimeter marker to zero each time they pass 10 centimeters.

GA1095

Pointing Out Measurement Facts

II

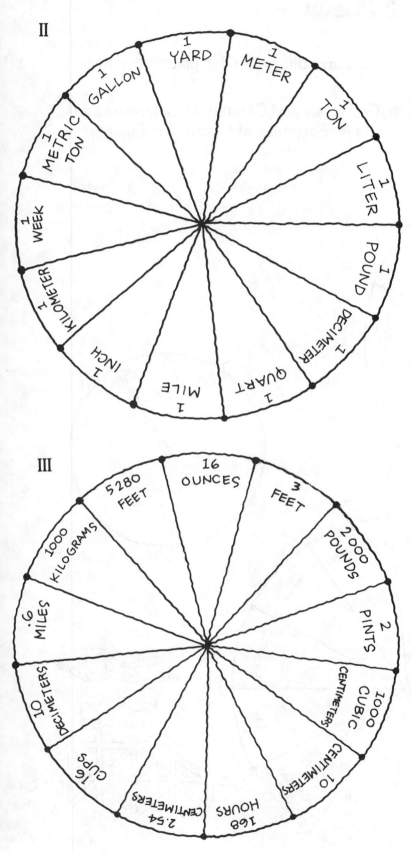

Cut out the small circle (I). Center the small wheel on the large wheel (II).

I

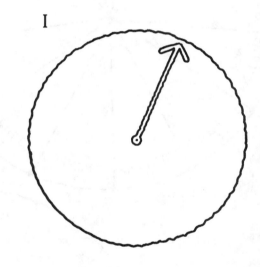

Listen for the problem your teacher calls out. Set the arrow to the correct answer. Repeat these directions for wheel (III).

III

GA1095

Pointing Out Measurement Facts
Blank Master

Ideas for the mathematics and general curriculum can be placed on these wheels:

● Multiplication ● Cities and States ● Countries and Capitals ● Scientists and Inventions ● Spelling Words ● Synonyms ● Formulas of Geometric Figures

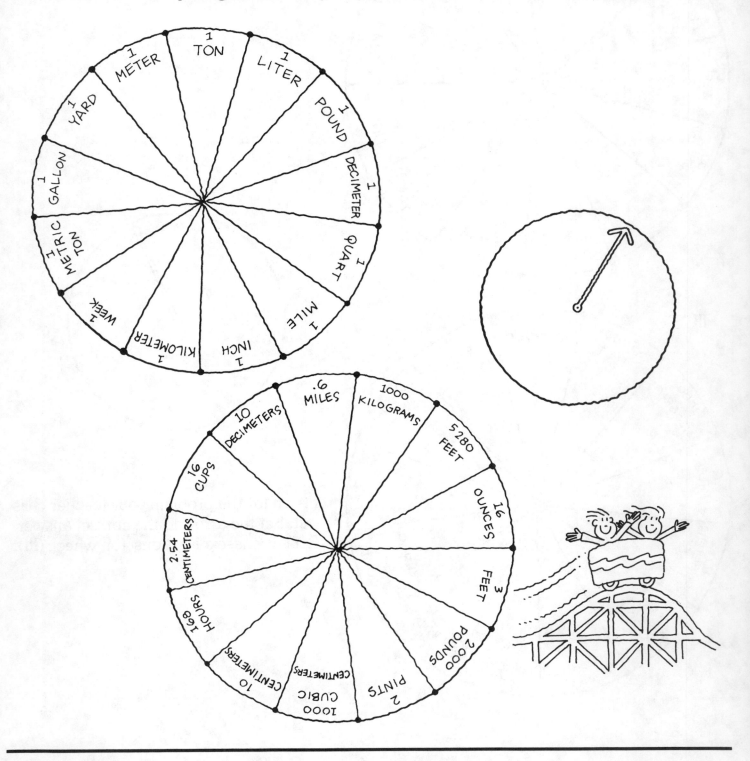

GA1095

Canadian
Mounted Police Patrol Map
To Be Used with Student Pages

☐ = 10 miles

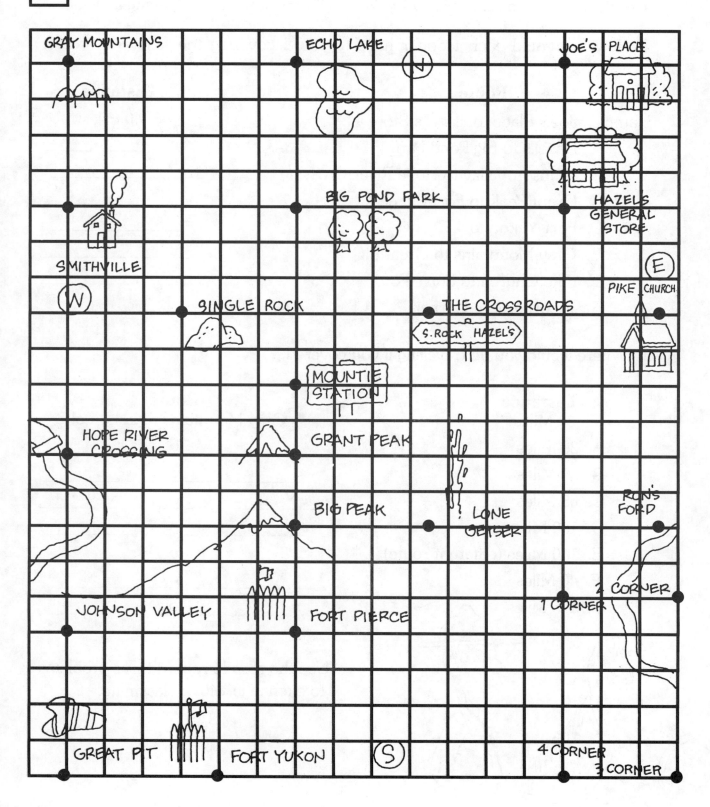

53

Canadian Mounted Police Patrol
Coverage Area Distance
Student Work Sheet

Major Fine assigns job routes for his Mounted Police troop. Each box is ten miles by ten miles (hint: 1 mile by 1 mile for primary students' beginning activities).

I. How far would each trooper have to travel covering the following areas?

Route	Distance
Example: Joe's Place to Hazel's Store	40 miles
A. Hazel's to Big Pond Park	_____
B. Johnson Valley to Hope River Crossing	_____
C. Grant Peak to Fort Pierce	_____
D. Fort Yukon to 4 Corner	_____
E. Gray Mountains to Great Pit	_____
F. Pike Church to Ron's Ford	_____
G. 1 Corner to 4 Corner	_____

II. Where would you be travelling if you covered. . . ?

Distance	Route
Example: 60 Miles	Gray Mountains to Echo Lake
A. 20 Miles	_____ to _____
B. 30 Miles	_____ to _____
C. 65 Miles	_____ to _____
D. 160 Miles	_____ to _____
E. 160 Miles (different route)	_____ to _____
F. 40 Miles	_____ to _____
G. 125 Miles	_____ to _____

Use the map to record three problems to exchange with a classmate.

GA1095

Canadian Mounted Police Patrol
Coverage Area Square Miles
Student Work Sheet

Major Fine knows you multiply *the length* of a Mountie's coverage times *the width* to find the total area covered (square miles).

I. How many square miles are involved in these routes?

Route	Distance	Square Miles
Example: All Four Corners	30 × 50 = 1500 square miles	
A. Gray Mountains/Echo Lake/Big Pond/ Smithville	_____ = _____	
B. Hope River/Grant Peak/Johnson Valley/Fort Pierce	_____ = _____	
C. Echo Lake/Big Pond/Hazel's/Joe's	_____ = _____	
D. Smithville/Hazel's/Joe's/Gray Mountains	_____ = _____	

II. How far is it around each of these same routes (perimeter)?

A.   C.

B.   D.

Major Fine knows that triangular areas can be found by multiplying the length times width and then dividing by two.

III. What is the area of these routes in square miles?

A. Johnson Valley/Great Pit/Fort Yukon   _____ = _____

B. 1 Corner/2 Corner/3 Corner   _____ = _____

C. Smithville/Hope River/Grant Peak   _____ = _____

D. Johnson Valley/Great Pit/3 Corner   _____ = _____

IV. Is there a shortcut for finding a

Mountie's triangular area?

GA1095

Canadian Mounted Police Patrol
Blank Master

   Imagine you are living in the wilderness during the 1800's. What would your territory look like? Design your territory, set your scale, and write five questions to exchange with a fellow frontier person.

☐ = 10 miles   **Territory Name**＿＿＿＿＿＿＿＿＿＿＿＿＿

Evaluate my territory before answering these questions.

1. ＿＿＿＿＿＿＿＿＿＿＿＿＿＿＿＿＿＿＿＿＿＿＿＿＿＿
2. ＿＿＿＿＿＿＿＿＿＿＿＿＿＿＿＿＿＿＿＿＿＿＿＿＿＿
3. ＿＿＿＿＿＿＿＿＿＿＿＿＿＿＿＿＿＿＿＿＿＿＿＿＿＿
4. ＿＿＿＿＿＿＿＿＿＿＿＿＿＿＿＿＿＿＿＿＿＿＿＿＿＿
5. ＿＿＿＿＿＿＿＿＿＿＿＿＿＿＿＿＿＿＿＿＿＿＿＿＿＿

GA1095

Measuring Likes and Dislikes

Have two of your classmates indicate the strength of their likes and dislikes by completing the line graphs below. Then complete a progressive line graph for each person in the space provided below.

	Hate	0	1	2	3	4	5	6	7	8	9	10	Love	Score
Example:	Liver I	•	•	•	•	•	•	•	•	•	•	•		____
	Liver II	•	•	•	•	•	•	•	•	•	•	•		____
	Spinach I	•	•	•	•	•	•	•	•	•	•	•		____
	Spinach II	•	•	•	•	•	•	•	•	•	•	•		____
	Pepsi I	•	•	•	•	•	•	•	•	•	•	•		____
	Pepsi II	•	•	•	•	•	•	•	•	•	•	•		____
	Ballet I	•	•	•	•	•	•	•	•	•	•	•		____
	Ballet II	•	•	•	•	•	•	•	•	•	•	•		____
	Sports I	•	•	•	•	•	•	•	•	•	•	•		____
	Sports II	•	•	•	•	•	•	•	•	•	•	•		____
	Bingo I	•	•	•	•	•	•	•	•	•	•	•		____
	Bingo II	•	•	•	•	•	•	•	•	•	•	•		____
	Books I	•	•	•	•	•	•	•	•	•	•	•		____
	Books II	•	•	•	•	•	•	•	•	•	•	•		____
	Math I	•	•	•	•	•	•	•	•	•	•	•		____
	Math II	•	•	•	•	•	•	•	•	•	•	•		____
	Movies I	•	•	•	•	•	•	•	•	•	•	•		____
	Movies II	•	•	•	•	•	•	•	•	•	•	•		____
	TV I	•	•	•	•	•	•	•	•	•	•	•		____
	TV II	•	•	•	•	•	•	•	•	•	•	•		____

#I's Average ____
#II's Average ____

GA1095

Measuring Likes and Dislikes

Student Design Page

Blank Master

Select ten categories for your like and dislike survey. Have two classmates share their preferences. Complete the progressive line graph below.

	Hate	0	1	2	3	4	5	6	7	8	9	10	Love	Score
_____	I.	•	•	•	•	•	•	•	•	•	•	•		_____
_____	II.	•	•	•	•	•	•	•	•	•	•	•		_____
_____	I.	•	•	•	•	•	•	•	•	•	•	•		_____
_____	II.	•	•	•	•	•	•	•	•	•	•	•		_____
_____	I.	•	•	•	•	•	•	•	•	•	•	•		_____
_____	II.	•	•	•	•	•	•	•	•	•	•	•		_____
_____	I.	•	•	•	•	•	•	•	•	•	•	•		_____
_____	II.	•	•	•	•	•	•	•	•	•	•	•		_____
_____	I.	•	•	•	•	•	•	•	•	•	•	•		_____
_____	II.	•	•	•	•	•	•	•	•	•	•	•		_____
_____	I.	•	•	•	•	•	•	•	•	•	•	•		_____
_____	II.	•	•	•	•	•	•	•	•	•	•	•		_____
_____	I.	•	•	•	•	•	•	•	•	•	•	•		_____
_____	II.	•	•	•	•	•	•	•	•	•	•	•		_____
_____	I.	•	•	•	•	•	•	•	•	•	•	•		_____
_____	II.	•	•	•	•	•	•	•	•	•	•	•		_____
_____	I.	•	•	•	•	•	•	•	•	•	•	•		_____
_____	II.	•	•	•	•	•	•	•	•	•	•	•		_____
_____	I.	•	•	•	•	•	•	•	•	•	•	•		_____
_____	II.	•	•	•	•	•	•	•	•	•	•	•		_____

```
10  • • • • • • • • • •
 9  • • • • • • • • • •
 8  • • • • • • • • • •
 7  • • • • • • • • • •
 6  • • • • • • • • • •
 5  • • • • • • • • • •
 4  • • • • • • • • • •
 3  • • • • • • • • • •
 2  • • • • • • • • • •
 1  • • • • • • • • • •
 0  • • • • • • • • • •
I (Red)   • • • • • • • • • •
II (Blue) • • • • • • • • • •
(Choices)
```

GA1095

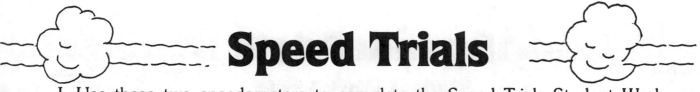

Speed Trials

I. Use these two speedometers to complete the Speed Trials Student Work Sheet. Place the given letters above the correct answers. Your teacher might also orally challenge you to use your pencil as the speedometer needle.

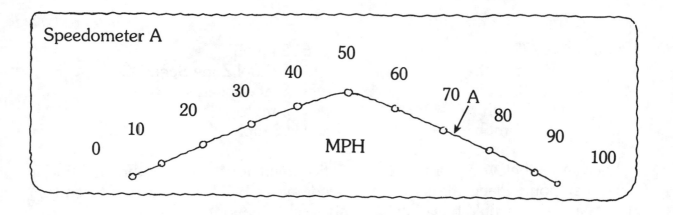

Speedometer A

50
40   60
30   70 A
20   80
10   90
0   100
            MPH

Teacher Hint: Change the MPH to kilometers per hour if necessary.

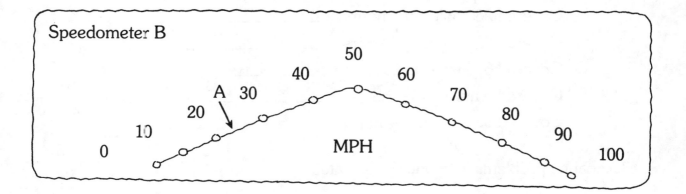

Speedometer B

50
40   60
A 30   70
20   80
10   90
0   100
            MPH

II. Write a humorous short story "The Fastest Car and Its Measurements."

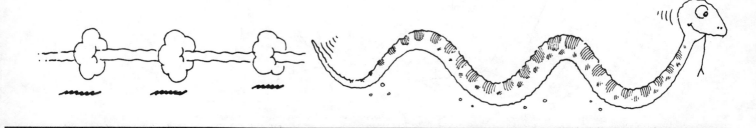

59

Speed Trials
Student Work Sheet

The letters below have miles per hour written next to them. Place the letters on Speedometer A. Use an arrow to show where the needle of the speedometer would point to show the miles per hour.

I.

Example:
A. 72 mph
B. 46 mph
C. 13 mph
D. 7 mph
E. 81 mph

F. 24 mph
G. School Zone Speed Limit
H. State Speed Limit
I. 3 mph
J. 92 mph

Each letter below has a mileage situation next to it. Answer the situation in miles per hour. Place the letter on Speedometer B. Use the arrow to show how fast the car would be going to satisfy each situation.

II.

Example: Covered 46 miles in 2 hours = 23 miles per hour

A. Covered 51 miles in 3 hours = _____

B. Covered 285 miles in 3 hours = _____

C. Covered 336 miles in 4 hours = _____

D. Covered 376 miles in 8 hours = _____

E. Covered 6 miles in 1½ hours = _____

F. Covered 63 miles in 2¼ hours = _____

Exchange problems with your classmates.

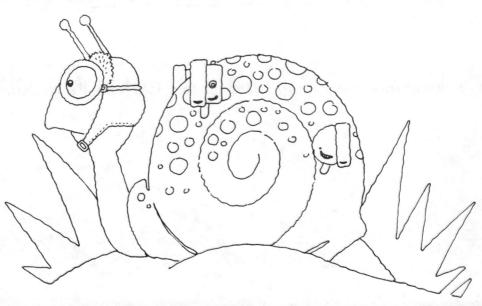

GA1095

Speed Trials

Teacher Directions

The *dials program* allows for great teacher flexibility. You can place a decimal point to the left of each number on the speedometer (.10) and create hundredths of an imaginary space travel measure called *kilohours* or place the decimal point in the middle for parts of *quasons*. After deciding what measure you are using, start the class with some basic find-the-location-of exercises (.17 or 1.7 or 17 miles per hour).

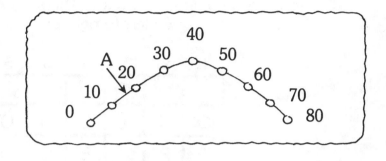

Place the speedometer on the chalkboard and use your pointer as a needle the same way students will use their pencils as the needle for their work sheets. Next ask the students to do some basic problems. A. (2 × .085 or 2 × .85 or 2 × 8.5, etc.) Tell them the letter to the left of the problem should now be placed above the correct answer on the speedometer dial. After doing a few problems, turn to the Speed Trials Student Work Sheet.

Problems can be adjusted to fit the various student abilities in the class. After the basics have been reviewed, a number of short-term projects can be incorporated into this unit.

I. Design a mini mileage chart showing the distance from your town to five neighboring towns. Show how long it will take at various speeds.

Philadelphia to:	Distance	55 mph	30 mph	10 mph
Harrisburg	90	1 hr. 40 min.	3 hours	9 hours
Scranton	120	2 hrs. 5 min.	4 hours	12 hours

II. Design a car of today or the future. Label the car's body measurements, speeds and turning radius.

III. Find the records of cars or horses at various racetracks around the country for the distance of one mile. Compute their winning time into miles per hour.

IV. Make a chart showing the speed of animals. Illustrate the animal with the speed under it (cheetah 60 mph).

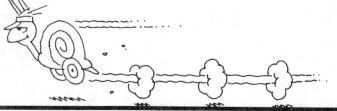

GA1095

Rhyme-a-Measure Word

Each line across the chart below contains a number of words. Two of the words rhyme. One of the two is a *measurement word*. Find and record the words below. The values above the starting letters for the words are multiplied. The words are written left to right or right to left.

	1	2	3	4	5	6	7	8	9	10	11	12	13
Example:	H	O	T	O	O	F	A	S	O	O	T	E	N
1.	O	N	I	S	U	O	C	N	E	Z	O	D	E
2.	T	R	E	E	C	N	U	O	B	A	L	U	H
3.	S	E	A	Q	U	A	R	T	R	O	P	E	G
4.	S	P	A	R	E	H	C	N	I	P	U	L	L
5.	N	O	W	E	I	G	H	T	T	I	A	B	E
6.	L	A	N	D	E	E	P	S	O	R	E	A	D
7.	O	F	F	A	K	E	R	C	A	R	T	O	P
8.	A	S	H	O	U	R	E	W	O	L	F	A	T
9.	P	L	E	A	Y	R	T	E	M	O	E	G	G
10.	A	V	O	L	U	M	E	S	A	T	O	M	B
11.	U	S	E	S	C	A	R	D	R	A	Y	E	S
12.	S	O	M	E	T	E	R	E	T	A	E	H	A

Example: <u>foot</u>   <u>soot</u>   6 x 8 = 48

1. ____ ____ ____

2. ____ ____ ____

3. ____ ____ ____

4. ____ ____ ____

5. ____ ____ ____

6. ____ ____ ____

7. ____ ____ ____

8. ____ ____ ____

9. ____ ____ ____

10. ____ ____ ____

11. ____ ____ ____

12. ____ ____ ____

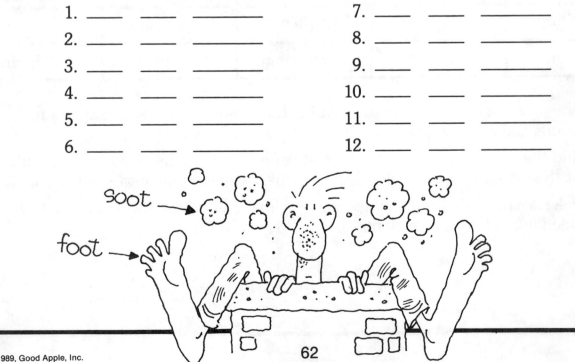

soot →

foot →

GA1095

Rhyme-a-Measure Word
Blank Master

Each line across the chart contains a number of words. Two of the words rhyme. Find them and record them below. The values above the starting letters for the words are multiplied. The words are written in both directions.

Teacher Hint: Historical figures in math/measurement can also be hidden. (NEWTON-SON, FURY-CURIE, DA VINCI-FREE) Save your student themes for future classes.

Theme _____

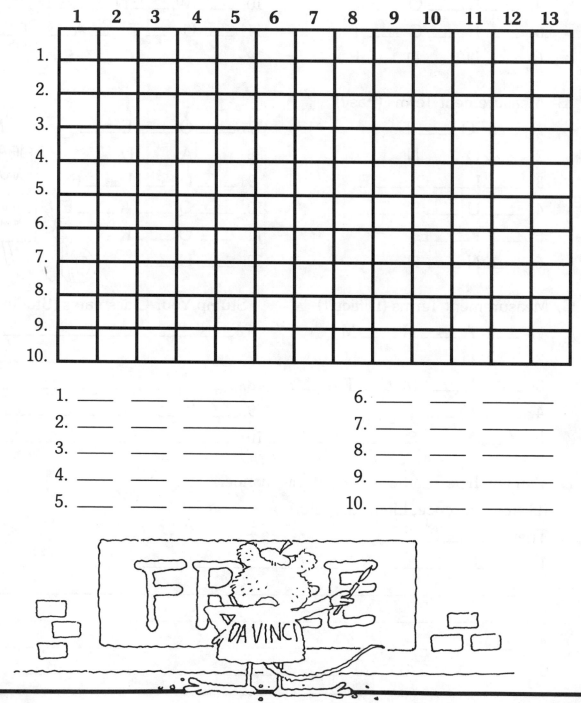

1. ___ ___ _____   6. ___ ___ _____
2. ___ ___ _____   7. ___ ___ _____
3. ___ ___ _____   8. ___ ___ _____
4. ___ ___ _____   9. ___ ___ _____
5. ___ ___ _____   10. ___ ___ _____

GA1095

Missing Measurement Vocabulary
Student Work Sheet

Each math and measurement word below has every other letter missing. How many answers can you find?

A. Math Terms

1. ___ U ___ B ___ R
2. ___ D ___ I ___ I ___ N
3. ___ Q ___ A ___
4. ___ E ___ O
5. ___ E ___ G ___ T
6. ___ U ___ D ___ E ___ S

7. ___ I ___ I ___ I ___ N
8. ___ R ___ C ___ I ___ N
9. ___ V ___ N
10. ___ W ___ N ___ Y
11. ___ U ___ T ___ A ___ T ___ O ___
12. ___ B ___ C ___ S

B. Measurement Terms (Easy)

1. ___ O ___ T
2. ___ O ___ N ___
3. ___ I ___ C ___ E
4. ___ U ___ E ___
5. ___ I ___ E
6. ___ N ___ H

7. ___ O ___ E ___
8. ___ A ___ D
9. ___ I ___ U ___ E
10. ___ Q ___ A ___ E
11. ___ O ___ R
12. ___ U ___

MISSING MEASUREMENT VOCABULARY

C. Measurement Terms (Difficult)

1. ___ A ___ H ___ M
2. ___ U ___ L ___ N ___
3. ___ E ___ M ___ T ___ Y
4. ___ C ___ E
5. ___ E ___ S ___ O ___ N

Stump Your Classmates (Student choices)

6. _____
7. _____
8. _____
9. _____
10. _____

D. Can you hide another theme in this manner?
(History, Science, Literature, etc.)

Theme _____

1. _____
2. _____
3. _____
4. _____
5. _____

GA1095

Missing Measurement Vocabulary
Teacher Directions

Place three of your students' names on the chalkboard in this form:
___E ___ N___I ___ (Jeannie), ___ O ___ E ___ T (Robert),
___I ___ D ___ (Cindy/Mindy). Ask the class to guess the identity of the
missing names. Explain that this same technique will now be used with math/
measurement words. The author likes dictating the words two at a time or playing
the class against the work sheet.

This technique can be used for all subject areas. It is modified when sentences
are involved.

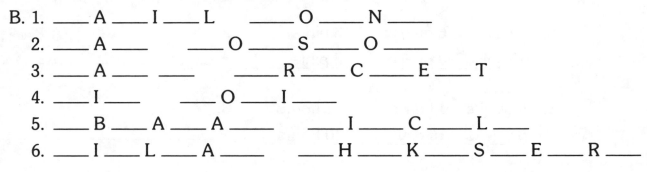

A. H ___ W   ___ A ___ Y   E ___ G ___   ___ R ___   ___ N
   S ___ X   ___ O ___ E ___?

Historical names are challenging in this form, also.

B. 1. ___ A ___ I ___ L   ___ O ___ N ___
   2. ___ A ___   ___ O ___ S ___ O ___
   3. ___ A ___ ___   ___ R ___ C ___ E ___ T
   4. ___ I ___   ___ O ___ I ___
   5. ___ B ___ A ___ A ___   ___ I ___ C ___ L ___
   6. ___ I ___ L ___ A ___   ___ H ___ K ___ S ___ E ___ R ___

GA1095

Measurement, Addition and Conversion Problems

Super Student Work Sheet

Your measurement and conversion knowledge will be challenged with this addition activity. Add the two measures and simplify your answer. In the column on the right, design a similar problem to share with a classmate.

Example:

3 hours	46 minutes	27 seconds
+ 8 hours	26 minutes	54 seconds
12 hours	13 minutes	21 seconds

Example:

+ _____

1.

10 m	13 dm	87 cm1.
+ 23 m	42 dm	35 cm

1.

+ _____

2.

8 gal.	6 quarts	8 pints
+ 10 gal.	3 quarts	8 pints

2.

+ _____

3.

5 weeks	13 days	18 hours
+ 6 weeks	16 days	10 hours

3.

+ _____

4.

6 yards	13 feet	22 inches
+ 8 yards	32 feet	41 inches

4.

+ _____

5.

7 inches	¾ inch	⅝ inch
+ 2 inches	¼ inch	⅞ inch

5.

+ _____

6.

14 gross	38 dozen	6 singles
+ 20 gross	12 dozen	8 singles

6.

+ _____

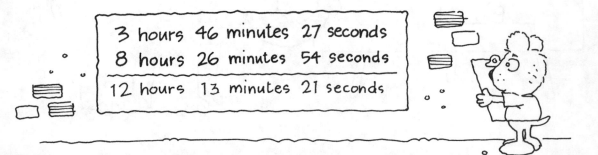

GA1095

andy Measures

Most textbooks will tell you how early measures were based on the size of the ruler's hand or foot. A new ruler meant a confusing change in the measuring system. To avoid this, measurement had to be standardized. What would have happened years ago if your hand was the standard of measure and how would your measure compare to a classmate's? Use the rulers below to measure the length and width of each of your fingers. Figure the span (pinky to thumb/hand stretched), also. Compare your chart to a friend's chart.

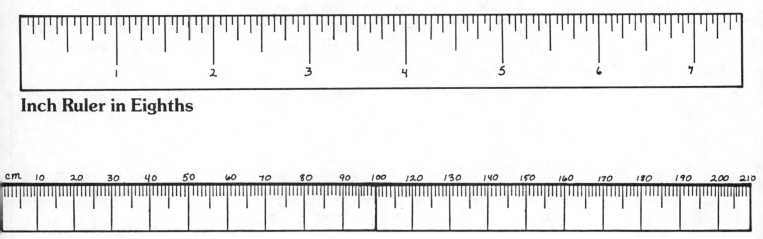

Inch Ruler in Eighths

Centimeter Ruler

Finger	Length	Width
A		
B		
C		
D		
E		
F (span)		

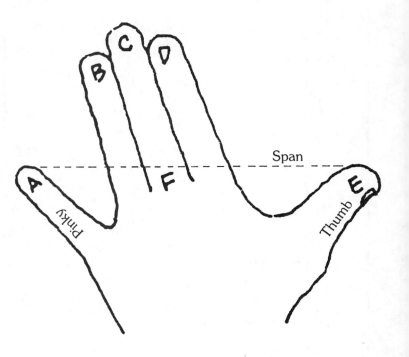

GA1095

Area of Rectangles and Triangles
Gameboard

Two teams or players alternate turns. Roll the dice and move to the geometric figure indicated by your roll. The width is missing. Roll your dice again. This roll is now the width. Place the figure's area in its middle and in your score column. Each roll eliminates a figure. Don't count it on future rolls. The winner is the person with the highest total after all the figures are claimed. Review your area formulas before starting this game.

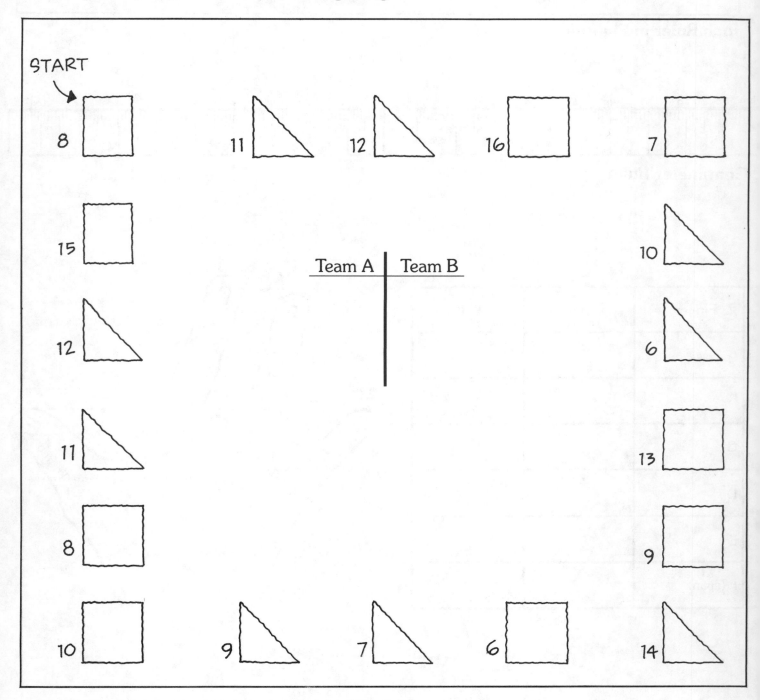

GA1095

Building Blocks of Area and Perimeter

Use these blocks to build structures below. Then fill in the area and perimeter of each structure in the chart below.

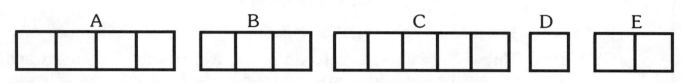

A   B   C   D   E

Build these structures by stacking the blocks below.

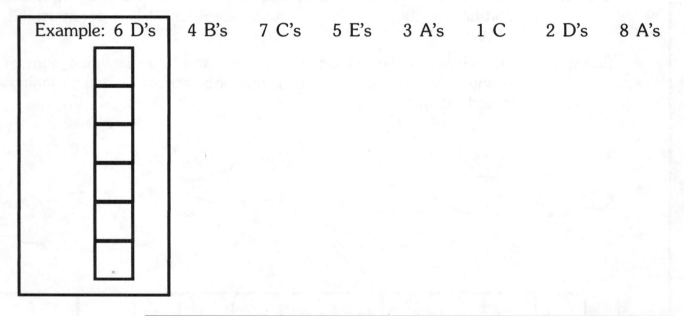

Example: 6 D's   4 B's   7 C's   5 E's   3 A's   1 C   2 D's   8 A's

	Drawing	Length	Width	Area	Perimeter
Example:	6D	6	1	6	14
1.	4B				
2.	7C				
3.	5E				
4.	3A				
5.	1C				
6.	2D				
7.	8A				

GA1095

Crossing Out Areas and Perimeters

Gameboard

Materials: Two number cubes (1, 2, 3, 4, 5, 6)

Object: Throw two cubes; select *one* of the two possible *outcomes* and color in the appropriate matching number on the activity board below.

Outcome: One cube is the length of the rectangle and the other is the width. You have a choice to cross out the area (L x W) or perimeter (2L + 2W).

Scoring: The winner is the person to cross out the last remaining number in any column. You could also total your scores over nine innings to find a winner.

1	2	3	4	5	6
8	9	10	12	14	15
16	18	20	22	24	25
30	36	4	5	6	8
9	10	12	14	15	16
18	20	22	24	25	30

Player 1

Player 2

GA1095

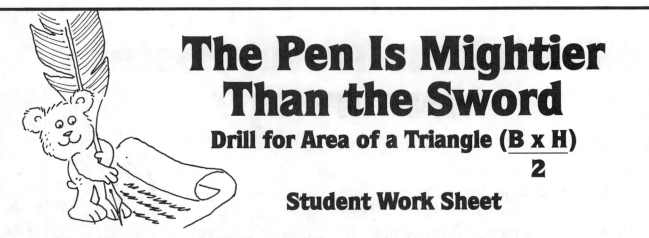

The Pen Is Mightier Than the Sword

Drill for Area of a Triangle $\frac{(B \times H)}{2}$

Student Work Sheet

The clues below will help you find words that have PEN in exact order written in them. Use the chart below to determine the value of your answer's first and last letters. Multiply these values and divide by two to find your score.

Clue	Answer	Letters ÷ 2	Score
Example: A writing tool	Pencil	P x L	$\frac{12 \times 9 = 54}{2}$
1. Polar animal	_____	_____ =	_____ =
2. Five-sided figure	_____	_____ =	_____ =
*3. To turn over	_____	_____ =	_____ =
4. Internal part of the body	_____	_____ =	_____ =
5. Rooftop apartment	_____	_____ =	_____ =
6. Necklace part	_____	_____ =	_____ =
7. Land mass	_____	_____ =	_____ =
8. Disease fighter	_____	_____ =	_____ =
9. Flag or banner	_____	_____ =	_____ =
10. Make amends for wrong	_____	_____ =	_____ =
11. Holds up pants	_____	_____ =	_____ =
12. Girl's name	_____	_____ =	_____ =
13. Not closed	_____	_____ =	_____ =
14. At a 90⁰ angle	_____	_____ =	_____ =

7	8	12	9	11
A F K O U Z	B G M Q V	C H P R W	D I S L X	E J N T Y

GA1095

Does Your Travel Poster Measure Up?

I. Design two travel posters attracting people to:

   a. your town or state
   b. favorite city or state
   c. a foreign country
   d. a tourist attraction (for example, the Statue of Liberty)
   e. an island or continent

II. Next to your poster place a route map showing the mileage from nearby cities, states or countries.

Attraction I	Mileage Map

Attraction II	Mileage Map

Teacher Hint: This activity looks fantastic on 11" x 14" art paper. Use this sheet for student planning.

GA1095

Back and Forth Measures
Student Work Sheet

Each *line* of the squares below can be read from left to right or right to left. If you put *them* in the correct order, you will create a *measurement* word.

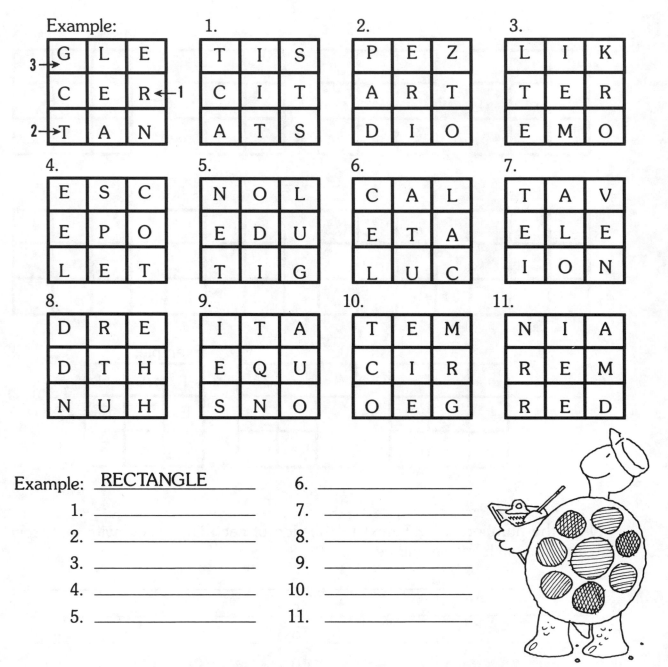

Example:

3→ G L E
C E R ←1
2→ T A N

1.
T I S
C I T
A T S

2.
P E Z
A R T
D I O

3.
L I K
T E R
E M O

4.
E S C
E P O
L E T

5.
N O L
E D U
T I G

6.
C A L
E T A
L U C

7.
T A V
E L E
I O N

8.
D R E
D T H
N U H

9.
I T A
E Q U
S N O

10.
T E M
C I R
O E G

11.
N I A
R E M
R E D

Example: __RECTANGLE__

1. _____
2. _____
3. _____
4. _____
5. _____
6. _____
7. _____
8. _____
9. _____
10. _____
11. _____

Design some of your own back and forths on the blank sheet that follows.

Place the numbers 1, 2 or 3 next to the side of each line showing what direction and what order those three letters should be read.

73

GA1095

Back and Forth Measures
Blank Master

Each line in the squares below can be read from left to right or right to left. If you place the lines in correct order, you will create a _____ word.

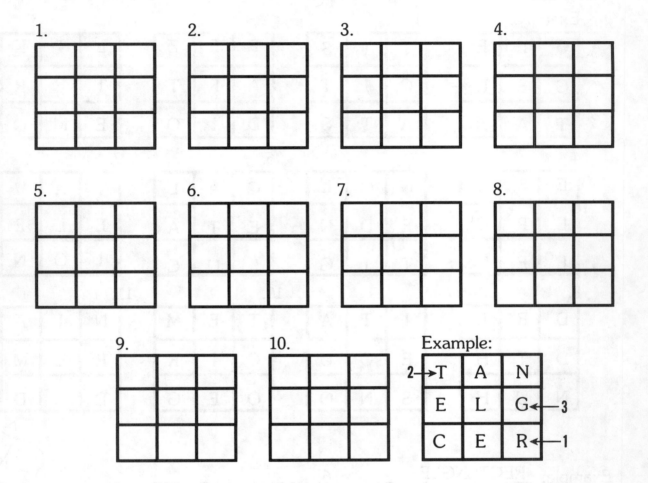

Place the numbers 1, 2, 3 next to the side of each line. Show with an arrow the direction each line should be read.

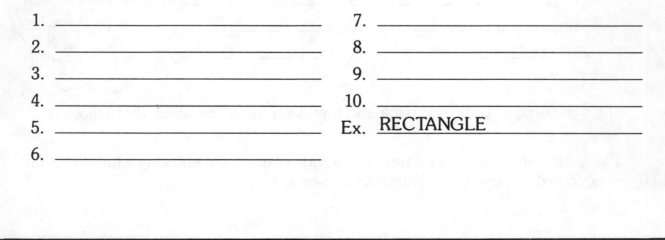

1. _____
2. _____
3. _____
4. _____
5. _____
6. _____

7. _____
8. _____
9. _____
10. _____
Ex. <u>RECTANGLE</u>

GA1095

Back and Forth Measures
Teacher Directions

Twenty percent of the problem-solving answers that students miss are caused by reading/vocabulary difficulties. Teaching mathematics vocabulary should be included in all math units, not just the measurement phase of the mathematics curriculum.

Place the following problems on the chalkboard:

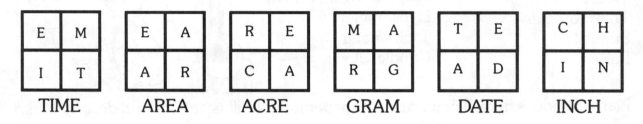

| TIME | AREA | ACRE | GRAM | DATE | INCH |

Tell the class each line can be read left to right or right to left. If the lines are read in the correct order, a math/measurement word can be found. Do one at a time until the class is ready for the next level of challenges. The author has students draw blank boxes and then dictates the challenges to the class one at a time.

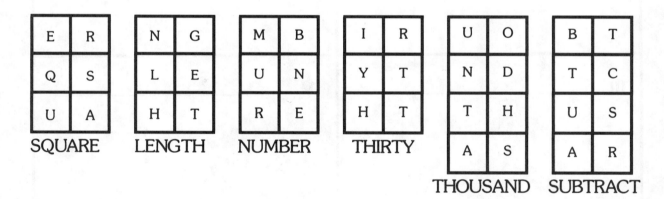

| SQUARE | LENGTH | NUMBER | THIRTY | THOUSAND | SUBTRACT |

Here are some additional words you might want to include before moving on to the student sheet.

| ADDEND | ABACUS | DIVIDE | TRIANGLE | OUNCES |
| FACTOR | ELEVEN | MULTIPLY | CENTIMETER | CIRCLE |

GA1095

Measurement Devices
Student Work Sheet

The study of measurement devices is also the study of mathematics, history, creative people and critical thinking. The world is full of *well-known* and *not-so-well-known*, yet important, measuring tools. Make a list of ten devices in each category; then illustrate and define the use of your four most unique devices.

Well-Known
Thermometer
Sundial
Ruler

Not-So-Well-Known
Hypsometer
Tachometer
Candle Clock

Plan your ideas here. Then use larger paper for your illustrations and descriptions.

I. _____

II. _____

III. _____

IV. _____

GA1095

Measurement Conversion Charts
Super Student Work Sheet

Your measurement IQ will be put to the ultimate test with these conversion charts. The measures on the left can be represented in an easier-to-understand format. See how many you can convert.

Example:

	Weeks	Days	Hours
1000 Hours	5	2	12

I.

	Weeks	Days	Hours
500 Hours			
1500 Hours			
2400 Hours			
215 Hours			

II.

	Miles	Feet
10,000 Feet		
20,000 Feet		
52,900 Feet		
10,570 Feet		

III.

	Tons	Lbs.	Ozs.
32,017 Ozs.			
64,000 Ozs.			
35,100 Ozs.			
10,000 Ozs.			

IV.

	Hours	Min.	Sec.
4000 Sec.			
8000 Sec.			
10,000 Sec.			
12,000 Sec.			

V.

	Gal.	Quarts	Pints
43 Pints			
86 Pints			
96 Pints			
302 Pints			

VI.

	Yards	Feet	Inches
65 Inches			
100 Inches			
250 Inches			
375 Inches			

GA1095

Measurement Magazine Cover

National Geographic magazine is celebrating its hundredth year of publishing by saluting our world past, present and future. You are to design a *National Geographic* book cover highlighting *Measurement and Its Discoverers*—past, present and future. Use the space below for your cover or complete it on larger paper. Remember to include a cover index and creative titles.

Teacher: Future covers could include *Time, Sports Illustrated*, etc. Create a hall display with each cover assignment.

The World of Measurement
Research Project Preplanner

1. What area of mathematics is the focus of your project?	2. How long will your project take to complete?
3. How does the study of measurement relate to your project?	4. Who might you contact by telephone for project information?
5. What question will your project answer?	6. What will your charts and graphs reflect?
7. What media will you use in your multimedia presentation? (posters, filmstrip, overhead transparency models, diorama)	8. What group might be interested in your findings?

Brief Description of Project

GA1095

Research Investigation Monitoring System

Date

1. Preresearch Planner	_____	fair	good	excellent
2. Phone Interview	_____	fair	good	excellent
3. Three Articles	_____	fair	good	excellent
4. References	_____	fair	good	excellent
5. Graphs	_____	fair	good	excellent
6. Note Cards	_____	fair	good	excellent
7. Outline	_____	fair	good	excellent
8. Final Format	_____	fair	good	excellent
9. Presentation	_____	fair	good	excellent

Research Title: _____

Question: _____

Name: _____   Grade: _____

Teacher: _____

80

GA1095

Measurement Project
Great Poets, Great Poems

Name of poet _____

Years lived _____ to _____

Selected titles _____

_____

_____

_____

_____

_____

_____

_____

_____

I. Brief biographical sketch of poet

_____

_____

_____

II. How is measurement important to poetry?

_____

_____

_____

Your original poem in the style of a selected title above

_____

_____

_____

_____

_____

_____

_____

Your name _____

GA1095

Measurement Project
Inventors and Their Inventions

Name of inventor _____

Years lived _____ to _____

Picture of Invention I

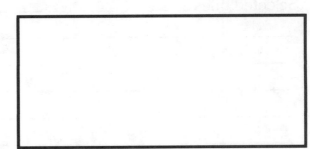

Picture of Invention II

I. Brief biographical sketch of inventor

_____

_____

_____

_____

II. How important is measurement in discovery?

_____

_____

_____

_____

III. Importance you place on invention

_____

_____

_____

_____

_____

_____

_____

Your name _____

GA1095

Measurement Project
Great Artists, Great Paintings

[blank box]

Your copy of artist's painting

1. Name of artist _____
2. Years lived _____ to _____
3. Names of paintings _____
   _____
   _____

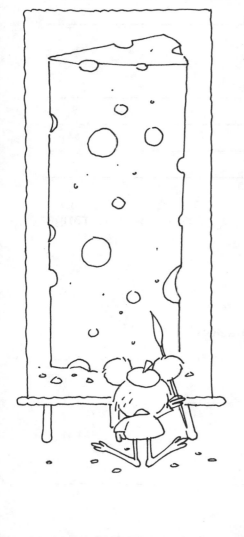

  I. Brief sketch of artist's life
   _____
   _____

  II. How is measurement important to art?
   _____
   _____
   _____

  III. Reasons you liked artist
   _____
   _____
   _____
   _____

      Your name _____

GA1095

Point of Vi w/Measur ment

Statement to be evaluated:

Is it necessary to learn measurement and how to measure when so many devices will do it for you?

Your point of view

_____
_____
_____
_____

Point of view of your group

_____
_____
_____
_____

Point of view opposite to what yours was

_____
_____
_____
_____

Teacher Hint: These following topics can be used to present a wide range of mathematical discussions:

1. Metric versus customary
2. Should math history be a part of mathematics class?
3. Should calculators be used on tests?

Have your students present their topics for future discussion.

Your name _____

GA1095

You Have Come a Long Way, Baby

Many measurement studies have been completed with infant birth facts. After completing these graphs you might want to begin an investigation of some of them. The first chart measures percent of weight increase while the second chart measures percent of height increase. Have eight friends find out their weight (in ounces) and height (in inches) at birth and now.

	Name	Birth Weight	Present Weight	*Percent Increase
1.				
2.				
3.				
4.				
5.				
6.				
7.				
8.				

*(PRESENT WEIGHT   BIRTH WEIGHT) x 100 = PERCENT INCREASE

	Name	Birth Height	Present Height	*Percent Increase
1.				
2.				
3.				
4.				
5.				
6.				
7.				
8.				

Record your facts and your friends' on the charts above.

GA1095

Baby Measurement Research

Baby studies focus on weight, height, intelligence and success as an adult. Pick one of these three types of births: premature, normal term or cesarean section. Tell what you discovered in the areas of height, weight, intelligence and future success. Ask your doctor or local health service for information.

Type of birth _____

Discoveries

Height

Weight

Intelligence

Success

GA1095

Nomination Form: Measurement Hall of Fame

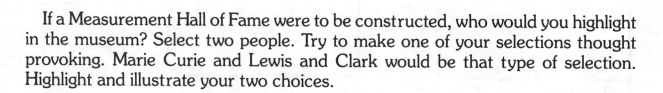

If a Measurement Hall of Fame were to be constructed, who would you highlight in the museum? Select two people. Try to make one of your selections thought provoking. Marie Curie and Lewis and Clark would be that type of selection. Highlight and illustrate your two choices.

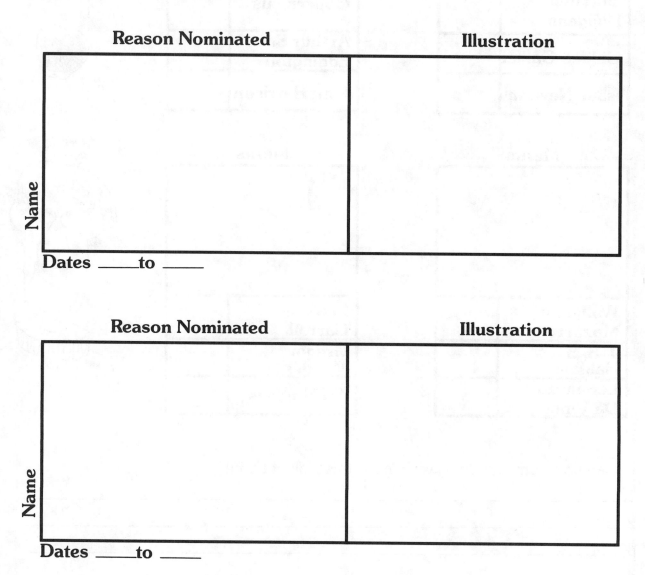

Reason Nominated   **Illustration**

Name

Dates _____ to _____

Reason Nominated   **Illustration**

Name

Dates _____ to _____

GA1095

Measurement Hall of Fame

Twelve people have been nominated for the Measurement Hall of Fame. Select one person from each group and explain why his accomplishments merit his entry into the Hall of Fame. Check your selection.

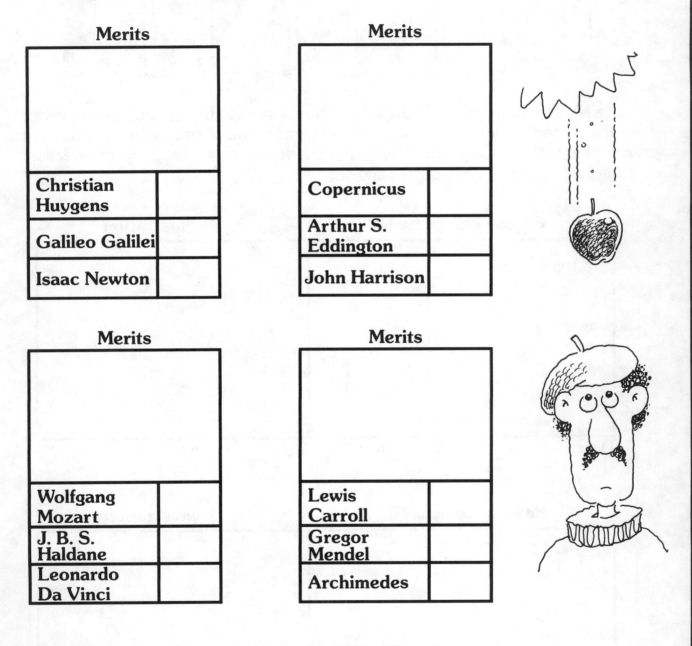

Merits

Christian Huygens	
Galileo Galilei	
Isaac Newton	

Merits

Copernicus	
Arthur S. Eddington	
John Harrison	

Merits

Wolfgang Mozart	
J. B. S. Haldane	
Leonardo Da Vinci	

Merits

Lewis Carroll	
Gregor Mendel	
Archimedes	

Can you nominate four women for this Hall of Fame?

1. _____

2. _____

3. _____

4. _____

GA1095

Women and Measurement

I. If you were to give a speech on "Women and Their Contributions to Measurement," who would be your selection for outstanding contributors? Place eight women and their "measured" contributions below. Highlight your outstanding contributors in the spaces below.

	Women	Areas of Contribution	Records
Example:	Amelia Earhart	Aviation	Solo Flights
1.			
2.			
3.			
4.			
5.			
6.			
7.			
8.			

II. Can you research two types of awards (Nobel Peace Prize/Philadelphia) and the percentage of women who have won them?

III. Outstanding Woman of Measurement.

Reason Selected	Depiction of the Event

Name

Dates_____to_____

GA1095

Olympic Measurements

Review the Olympic events and the variety of measurements that are involved from weight lifting, shooting, swimming/diving to track and field. Design two unique events of your own (real or humorous like the twenty-four-hour shopping spree or 20 centimeter bowler hat throw). Stress the measurement involved in each event and design the medal that will be awarded at its conclusion.

Name

Description

Illustration

Name

Description

Illustration

Use colored pencils to design the awards for each event. Transfer this page to 11" x 14" drawing paper.

Ribbon

Medal

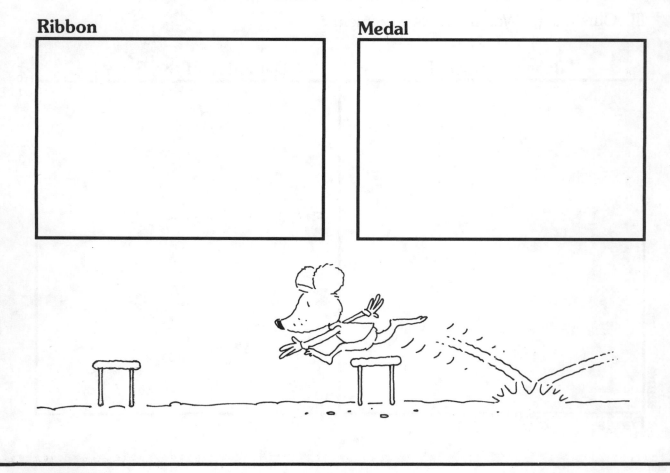

GA1095

Answer Key

nous Measurements I Page 9

984 ft.	4. 8981 ft.	7. 167 ft.
481 ft.	5. 4000 mi.	8. 1472 ft.
29,028 ft.	6. 555 ft.	9. 20,320 ft.

Time Trials Page 15

A. 1620
F. 1776
G. 1812
H. 1903
I. 1969
J. 1941
K. 1927

The Prize Is Right Page 18

	Area	Circumference
1.	113.04	37.68
2.	530.66	81.64
3.	1808.64	150.72
4.	12.56	12.56
5.	1017.36	113.04
6.	314.0	62.8
7.	28.26	18.84
8.	78.5	31.4
9.	153.86	43.96
10.	254.34	56.52

Rollover, Love and Hate Measurement Graphs Page 26

1. pullover, 8
2. shatters, 16
3. glove, 15
4. louvre, 24
5. theater, 35
6. Mad Hatter, 54
7. slovenly, 56
8. Hecate, 48
9. chatter, 63
10. lovely, 60
11. Wheaties, 88
12. louvered, 96
13. chapter, 91
14. threaten, 112
15. four-leaf clover, 210
16. cheater, 112

Metric Words Page 28

1. California = .5, .5, .7
2. Yugoslavia = .5, .5, .6
3. Kristopher = .3, .7, .5
4. Bernadette = .4, .6, .7
5. Harrisburg = .3, .7, .3
6. Automobile = .6, .4, .6
7. Washington = .3, .7, .7
8. Presidents .3, .7, .5
9. Newspapers = .3, .7, .5
10. Revolution = .5, .5, .6
11. Basketball = .3, .7, .7
12. Thermostat = .3, .7, .7

a. Strengthen
b. Understand
c. Steamboats
d. Television

Multiply Then Order Page 29

1. 18	2. 45	3. 90	4. 16
15	64	98	24
27	52	81	12
20	48	104	32
12	54	96	28
24	36	88	18
16	50	100	25
22	42	102	20

1. So far you seem to be doing well.
2. Yes, these problems are getting harder to do.
3. Are you having any trouble with your answers?
4. Was the easiest one saved for the end?

The Decimal Ruler Page 33
A. .73 B. .81 C. .69 D. .93

Words Worth an Inch Page 34

I. L = .60 or $60/100$ D = .20 or $20/100$ J = .50 or $50/100$
R = .85 or $85/100$ P = .80 or $80/100$ E = .25 or $25/100$

II.
L = .60	B = .10	G = .35	H = .40
O = .75	E = .25	O = .75	A = .05
V = .20	S = .05	L = .60	R = .85
E = .25	T = .10	F = .30	D = .20
1.80	.50	2.00	1.50

Metric Meter Reader/Jumps Page 46

I. B. 2, 1, 2
C. 4, 7, 0
D. 8, 4, 0
E. 4, 0, 0
F. 0, 8, 0
G. 0, 1, 2
H. 0, 7, 4
I. 1, 5, 5

II. B. 7301
C. 1220
D. 133
E. 1776
F. 2454

Yard Measure Drill Page 48

I. A. 1, 1
B. 2, 11
C. 0, 9
D. 1, 0
E. 2, 4
F. 6, 0
G. 24, 0

II. A. 147
B. 146
C. 71
D. 302
E. 343
F. 585

Canadian Mounted Police Patrol Page 54

I. A. 70
B. 50
C. 50
D. 90
E. 200
F. 60
G. 50

II. A. Grant Peak to Big Peak
B. 1 Corner to 2 Corner
C. Single Rock to Crossroads
D. Smithville to Great Pit
E. Hazel's to 4 Corner
F. Fort Yukon to Great Pit
G. Single Rock to Pike Church

Canadian Mounted Police Patrol Page 55

I. A. 60 × 40 = 2400 sq. mi.
B. 60 × 50 = 3000 sq. mi.
C. 40 × 70 = 2800 sq. mi.
D. 40 × 130 = 5200 sq. mi.

II. A. 200 miles
B. 220 miles
C. 220 miles
D. 340 miles

III. A. $\frac{40 \times 40}{2}$ = 800 sq. mi.

B. $\frac{30 \times 50}{2}$ = 750 sq. mi.

C. $\frac{70 \times 60}{2}$ = 2100 sq. mi.

D. $\frac{160 \times 40}{2}$ = 3200 sq. mi.

IV. Take half of rectangular area.

Speed Trials Page 60

A. 17 mph
B. 95 mph
C. 84 mph
D. 49 mph
E. 4 mph
F. 28 mph

GA1095

Rhyme-a-Measure Word Page 62

1. Dozen, Cousin, $12 \times 7 = 84$
2. Ounce, Bounce, $9 \times 9 = 81$
3. Quart, Port, $4 \times 11 = 44$
4. Inch, Pinch, $9 \times 10 = 90$
5. Weight, Bait, $3 \times 12 = 36$
6. Speed, Read, $8 \times 11 = 88$
7. Acre, Faker, $3 \times 9 = 27$
8. Hour, Flower, $3 \times 11 = 33$
9. Geometry, Plea, $1 \times 12 = 12$
10. Volume, Tomb, $2 \times 10 = 20$
11. Yard, Card, $11 \times 5 = 55$
12. Meter, Heater, $3 \times 12 = 36$

Missing Measurement Vocabulary Page 64

A.
1. Number
2. Addition
3. Equal
4. Zero
5. Weight/Height
6. Hundreds
7. Division
8. Fraction
9. Even
10. Twenty
11. Subtraction
12. Abacus

B.
1. Foot
2. Pound
3. Circle
4. Ruler
5. Mile/Time
6. Inch
7. Dozen
8. Yard
9. Minute
10. Square
11. Hour
12. Cup/Sum

C.
1. Fathom
2. Furlong
3. Geometry
4. Acre
5. Teaspoon

Missing Measurement Vocabulary Page 65

A. How many eggs are in six dozen?

B.
1. Daniel Boone
2. Sam Houston
3. Davy Crockett
4. Jim Bowie
5. Abraham Lincoln
6. William Shakespeare

Measurement, Addition and Conversion Problems Page 66

1. 39 m 7 dm 2 cm
2. 22 gal. 1 qt. 0 pts.
3. 15 weeks 2 days 4 hours
4. 30 yds. 2 ft. 3 in.
5. 11 in. — ⅜ in.
6. 38 gross 3 doz. 2 singles

Building Blocks of Area and Perimeter Page 69

1. 4, 3, 12, 14
2. 7, 5, 35, 24
3. 5, 2, 10, 14
4. 4, 3, 12, 14
5. 5, 1, 5, 12
6. 2, 1, 2, 6
7. 8, 4, 32, 24

The Pen Is Mightier Than the Sword Page 71

1. Penguin, $P \times N = \dfrac{12 \times 11}{2} = 66$

2. Pentagon, $P \times N = \dfrac{12 \times 11}{2} = 66$

3. Upend, $U \times D = \dfrac{7 \times 9}{2} = 31\frac{1}{2}$

4. Appendix, $A \times X = \dfrac{7 \times 9}{2} = 31\frac{1}{2}$

5. Penthouse, $P \times E = \dfrac{12 \times 11}{2} = 66$

6. Pendant, $P \times T = \dfrac{12 \times 11}{2} = 66$

7. Peninsula, $P \times A = \dfrac{12 \times 7}{2} = 42$

8. Penicillin, $P \times N = \dfrac{12 \times 11}{2} = 66$

9. Pennant, $P \times T = \dfrac{12 \times 11}{2} = 66$

10. Penance, $P \times E = \dfrac{12 \times 11}{2} = 66$

11. Suspenders, $S \times S = \dfrac{9 \times 9}{2} = 40\frac{1}{2}$

12. Penelope, $P \times E = \dfrac{12 \times 11}{2} = 66$

13. Open, $O \times N = \dfrac{7 \times 11}{2} = 38\frac{1}{2}$

14. Perpendicular, $P \times R = \dfrac{12 \times 12}{2} = 72$

Back and Forth Measures Page 73

1. Statistic
2. Trapezoid
3. Kilometer
4. Telescope
5. Longitude
6. Calculate
7. Elevation
8. Hundredth
9. Equations
10. Geometric
11. Remainder

Measurement Conversion Charts Page 77

I. 2, 6, 20
   8, 6, 12
   14, 2, 0
   1, 6, 3

II. 1, 4720
    3, 4160
    10, 100
    2, 10

III. 1, 1, 1
     2, 0, 0
     1, 193, 12
     0, 625, 0

IV. 1, 6, 40
    2, 13, 20
    2, 46, 40
    3, 20, 0

V. 5, 1, 1
   10, 3, 0
   12, 0, 0
   37, 3, 0

VI. 1, 2,5
    2, 2, 4
    6, 2, 10
    10, 1, 3

GA1095